A Century of **HONESTY, ENERGY, ECONOMY, SYSTEM**

A Century of HONESTY, ENERGY, ECONOMY, SYSTEM

Wentworth Institute of Technology, 1904-2004

JOSEPH P. CLIFFORD

Published by Wentworth Institute of Technology

Copyright © 2003 by Wentworth Institute of Technology

For information, address:

Wentworth Institute of Technology
Publications Office
550 Huntington Avenue
Boston, MA 02115

Written by Joseph P. Clifford

Designed by Jeannet Leendertse

Printed by Reynolds-DeWalt Printing Inc.

Bound by Acme Bookbinding

Library of Congress Control Number: 2003113789

Printed in the U.S.A.

First Printing

To my four leading ladies, Lynne, Julia, Jane, and Laura,
and to Peter, whom I just met.

Contents

ACKNOWLEDGEMENTS

Many sources contributed to my understanding of Wentworth Institute of Technology and its 100-year history. Two invaluable contributors were Jane Kelley, director of publications, who's a fantastic editor and boss, and Robert Zagarella, publications coordinator, who's a great colleague and an excellent writer (he authored the football piece on Pages 78-81). The book owes so much to the graphic design skills of Jeannet Leendertse. She is a bookmaking magician. This book would not have been possible without the professionalism and expertise of Wentworth librarian, Mary Ellen Flaherty, who made the maintenance of institutional archives a priority when she arrived here 18 years ago. Her stamp is on every single page of this book. Special thanks to Donald C. Main, vice president for development, and President John F. Van Domelen, for their support and leadership in making this book a reality. Thanks also to Dick Burtt, assistant to the president, for sealing my fate when he allowed me to make Dr. H. Russell Beatty the cover story of the Spring 1997 Alumni News magazine. I appreciate the trails blazed by previous Wentworth historians, Professor Alan Cleeton and Professor Amos St. Germain; they offered me many insights. A highlight of the research phase occurred on October 11, 2001, when I spent the day with Ed Wentworth of Dover, New Hampshire. Ed, like his distant cousin, Arioch, is descended from Elder William Wentworth. As the Wentworth family historian, he led me on a tour of Dover and Rollinsford, N.H., that was essential to my understanding of Arioch's upbringing. The staff of Boston Public Library's Microtext Department aided me several times in researching newspaper accounts from the early 20th century. A special debt of gratitude to my wife, Lynne, who thinks I don't listen to her editorial advice, but I always do. And thanks to my three beautiful girls, Julia, Jane, and Laura, who have lived uncomplainingly alongside 20 boxes of yellowed documents for the past two years. The most essential sources for the book, however, were the hundreds of alumni, students, professors, staff members, administrators, trustees, and friends whom I have interviewed during the past 10 years. I can't name them all, but special mention should be made of Joe Antocci, George Balich, Robert Beatty, Keith Berube, Ron Betts, Luther Blount, Nick Boas, Bob Boyden, Phil Brooks, Gail Tansey Catanzaro, Paul Cherkas, George Chryssis, Charlie Cimino, Phil Comeau, Hal Conner, Lee Conrad, Barry Couto, Charlie Creekmore, Ernest Crie, Richard Currier, Bob DeFelice, Jack Duggan, Clarence Earley, Robert Edwards, Jane Estella-Minias, Kevin Fuchs, Steve Fusi, David Gannon, James Garvin, George and Carol Gay, Bill Gorman, George Gramatikas, John Heinstadt, Tina Hetherton, Ryan Hutchins, Albert Jourdan, Maureen Keefe, Ted Kirkpatrick, Ann Kolakowski, Stephen Kustan, Dan Lanneville, Boyd Leslie, Howard Levine, Chris Levy, Patricia Lillis, Chad Lyons, Nanci McKeen-Booth, Willard Merrill, Jack Nelson, Frank Nestor, Lou Nichols (Frederick Dobbs' grandson), Carl Nickerson, Ed O'Leary, Charlie Pheeney, Paul Pisano, Sylvia Price, Doug Schumann, Raina and Bill Sturtz, Barbara Such, Carl Swanson, J. Gerin Sylvia, Ray Tavares, Arthur Thompson, Peter Tsokanis, John Van Domelen, John Vetere, Bob Villanucci, David Wahlstrom, Sinclair Weeks Jr., Bill Westland, Bill Whelan, Alan Whittemore, and Irene McSweeney Woodfall.

And thanks, of course, to the thousands of people who have studied, taught, and worked at Wentworth Institute of Technology during the past 100 years. I hope you enjoy reading the history you helped create.

The following publications and written work provided valuable information:
- Administration scrapbooks, 1911 to 1928;
- Alumni magazines, 1921 to present day;
- Annual Reports, 1925 to present day;
- *By the Year 2000* strategic plan;
- *By the Year 2007* strategic plan;
- Commencement programs, 1928 to present day;
- Course catalogs, 1911-12 to present day;
- Factbooks, 1980 to present day;
- Student Handbooks, 1924 to present day;
- Student newspapers (Wenitech/Spectrum/Transcript/Leopard Print), 1953 to present day;
- Tekton yearbooks, 1933 to present day;
- Wentworth Institute Bulletins, 1957 to 1966;
- World War I Honor Roll;
- Correspondence of Kenrick Baker, Frederick Dobbs, Paul B. Watson, Arioch Wentworth, Arthur Williston, and others;
- Estate of Arioch Wentworth;
- Memoranda of principals, presidents, trustees, faculty, and staff, 1911 to present day;
- Minutes of the Wentworth Alumni Association, 1913 to present day;
- *Beyond the Horizon of Science*, by Arthur Williston;
- *The Big Dig*, by Dan McNichol;
- *Dear Mr. Hunter: The Letters of Vojtech Preissig to Dard Hunter*;
- *Engineering the New South*, by Robert McMath;
- *History of 101st Engineers Regiment;*
- *John Volpe: The Life of an Immigrant's Son*, by Kathleen Kilgore;
- *School Architecture: Principles and Practices*, by John J. Donovan;
- Boston Globe newspaper, March 1903, November 1908;
- Boston Post newspaper, March 1903, November 1908;
- Boston Transcript newspaper, September 1912;
- Boston Landmarks Commission reports;
- Boston Redevelopment Authority, 1890 Bromley Atlas;
- "A Sketch of the Life of Arioch Wentworth," by William H. Wentworth;
- "Arioch Wentworth's Citadel," by James Jeas;
- "Gridiron Glory Days," by Robert Zagarella, Wentworth Magazine, Winter 2001;
- "Sharp Students Land Exciting Jobs," by Patricia Lillis, Wentworth Alumni News, Spring 1994;
- "Succeeding from Scratch," by Willard Merrill;
- "The Technical Institute in America," by Arthur Williston.

1904

2004

A Century of Honesty, Energy, Economy, System

Wentworth Institute of Technology, 1904-2004

April 5, 2004, marks the 100th anniversary of the founding of Wentworth Institute of Technology.

It's not reaching 100 years that's special: after all, half of the 46 colleges in Boston and Cambridge are older than a century. Rather, it's what gets accomplished along the way.

And in this regard, Wentworth's story is every bit as compelling as those of its collegiate brethren in the region.

Wentworth Institute of Technology came into being because one man, Arioch Wentworth, felt so strongly about education in the mechanical arts that he invested 5.4 million dollars to furnish it. (That's comparable to 106 million in today's dollars. The gift was later halved after a settlement with heirs who disputed the will.)

Lofty a figure as that was, when one considers what the school has accomplished during the past 100 years, it's hard to imagine a better return on investment.

The school's accomplishments have been guided by an adherence to the four principles that Arioch Wentworth believed were essential to personal and business excellence: honesty, energy, economy, and system.

In this history, we'll chart these accomplishments as we navigate through the years at Wentworth Institute of Technology—from the tone-setting leadership of Arthur Williston to the rock-solid stewardship of Frederick Dobbs; from the farsighted vision of Russ Beatty to the landmark changes enacted by Ted Kirkpatrick; from the renaissance sparked by John Van Domelen to the great opportunities that await Wentworth as it begins its second century as a leader in engineering technology education.

Along the way, we'll spotlight 15 outstanding days on the historical calendar. We'll honor the special service Wentworth has rendered to its nation during wartime. We'll pay tribute to 50 important players in the Wentworth story. We'll visit neighbors alongside whom Wentworth has lived, more or less peacefully, for the past 100 years. We'll look at the men and women who've walked through the halls of Wentworth Institute of Technology, what they found when they got here, and what they left behind. We'll remember long days and grueling classes, hard-fought games and never-forgotten lessons, first-generation college students and five-decade-long employees.

Above all, we'll celebrate a school that for the past century has served, and continues to serve, its students, its alumni, its nation, and the memory of its founder, very well indeed.

1904

WENTWORTH INSTITVTE
FOVNDED BY
ARIOCH WENTWORTH
FOR THE PVRPOSE OF FVRNISHINC
EDVCATION IN THE MECHANICAL ARTS

1904

THE SCHOOL'S FOUNDER: ARIOCH WENTWORTH

One sentence, 36 words long, brought Wentworth Institute to life 100 years ago. The school was launched not with high-flung rhetoric or philosophical entreaties, but instead through these simple and direct words found in the 11th paragraph of Arioch Wentworth's will:

"As soon as may be after my death [the trustees] shall, unless I have already done so, organize a corporation to be known as the Wentworth Institute, for the purpose of furnishing education in the mechanical arts."

This directive, added to his will a mere seven weeks before he died, represented the only firsthand account of Arioch Wentworth's interest in such an educational enterprise.

At first it seems odd that this school, which would go on to embody a solid, no-nonsense, hands-on philosophy, was founded in such an impetuous manner, seemingly on the whim of a dying 89-year-old man. But a closer look shows that Wentworth Institute was in fact no whim, but the fitting legacy of a 19th-century man blessed with 20th-century foresight.

Top left: Arioch Wentworth, 1813-1903.

Left: An inscription dedicated to the founder, part of a memorial that stood for many years on Huntington Avenue, across from the Museum of Fine Arts.

Below: A portion of Arioch Wentworth's last will and testament, written on January 22, 1903. His charitable interests reflected closely his formative years and his experience as an industrialist who succeeded despite the lack of an advanced education. Two bequests founded a nursing home and a hospital a quarter-mile from his Somersworth, New Hampshire, birthplace. Several others supported existing educational institutions, such as MIT and Bates College. The grandest of all set up the Institute he envisioned as a life-altering opportunity for the young tradesmen who labored in his Boston marble firm.

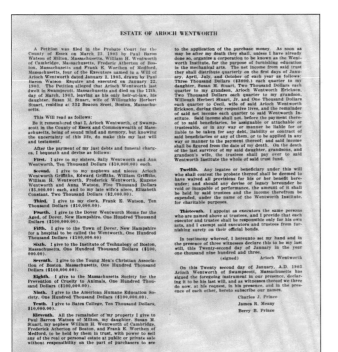

By most any means with which one cares to measure, Arioch Wentworth enjoyed a successful life. As a businessman, he crested the surging waves of two industries; as a landlord, he managed 50 lucrative properties in Boston; and as a philanthropist, he bestowed his large fortune to family members and an array of pet causes.

But he also wrestled with disappointment during his lifetime, professionally and personally. Arioch's first job, according to his nephew, William Hall Wentworth, dead-ended after four years because he lacked the training that would enable him to profit from his "unusual mechanical ability." Much later, a feud with his daughter's second husband caused deep family rifts. These two disappointments combined to provide ample motive for the founding of Wentworth Institute in 1904.

Right: A 1920 photograph of the house where Arioch Wentworth was born in 1813. His father built the house on the expansive family farm in Somersworth, New Hampshire.

Bottom left: The house today, on Route 4 in Rollinsford, N.H. (the town's name changed in 1849).

Bottom right: An engraved plate on a wrought-iron gate outside the family home reads, "Wentworth Manor, A.D. 1652." Above it is the distinctive Wentworth family crest.

Heroic Ancestors

Arioch Wentworth was born on June 13, 1813, in Somersworth, New Hampshire, just over the Dover line. (The town is known as Rollinsford today.) He grew up on the homestead that his family had owned since 1652.

Arioch's great-great-great grandfather, Elder William Wentworth, was born in Alford, England, in 1615, and sailed over to the Massachusetts colony in 1636. He soon associated himself with a group that followed Anne Hutchinson and Reverend John Wheelwright. In short time, they became embroiled in one of the most infamous controversies of colonial Massachusetts.

Hutchinson and Wheelwright preached a belief system that claimed followers could "experience continuing personal revelations from God." In the eyes of the prevailing Puritan church, this meant nothing less than heresy. After a sensational trial in May 1637, the followers of Hutchinson and Wheelwright were given four months to leave the colony.

Two months later, Elder William Wentworth sailed north to Exeter, New Hampshire. He moved from place to place until 1652, when he settled on the Somersworth farmland. There he became not just a farmer and a patriarch, but a hero as well.

A plaque affixed to a large rock on the Wentworth homestead pays tribute to Arioch Wentworth's distinguished ancestors: Elder William Wentworth, who sailed over from England in 1615, and three generations of gubernatorial uncles.

In 1689, Indians raided Dover and killed, wounded, and captured hundreds of settlers. The toll would have been worse had it not been for the actions of Wentworth. He was staying, along with many other townfolk, at the Heard Garrison House. A local history recounted how 74-year-old Wentworth single-handedly saved the garrison: "He was awakened by the barking of a dog, just as the Indians were entering. He pushed them out, and falling on his back, set his feet against the gate and held it till he had alarmed the people. Two balls were fired through the gate but both narrowly missed him."

Elder William's offspring would continue this legacy of service. He and his wife had nine sons. The oldest, Samuel, was grandfather to the first of three generations of Wentworth royal governors who ruled New Hampshire for 60 years until the American Revolution ended the King's reign in the colonies. William's youngest son, Benjamin, inherited the Somersworth homestead.

In 1788, the birth of Benjamin's great-grandson, Bartholomew, marked the fifth generation to grace the family farm. Bart grew into a strong man (he's called "gigantic" in a family history), who took over the homestead in 1813, two years after marrying his cousin, Nancy Hall. Together they raised seven children on the farm. The oldest was named Arioch.

Days of Soapstone and Marble

Arioch Wentworth enjoyed a happy childhood. When not being schooled at the Dover Academy, he worked hard on the family farm. He also earned money as a teacher's assistant and spent a lot of time laboring at a nearby granite quarry. By all accounts, he was mechanically gifted. In 1831, his father offered to send him to Dartmouth College to study law. Arioch declined, his nephew wrote, "as the prizes to be won in business seemed more desirable."

So, two years later, the 20-year-old departed for Boston, 90 miles south. In his first job, he helped build a wharf in the great port city. He was uncommonly industrious. One account related that jealous coworkers splashed his axe with seawater in hopes of causing it to rust. After four years, however, he walked away from this job, frustrated by his inability to turn his vaunted mechanical skills to higher, and more lucrative, ends.

Far right: Arioch's stern father, Bartholomew Wentworth. After Bart inherited the farm that his great-great grandfather, Elder William Wentworth, had purchased in 1652, he ran it masterfully for six decades.

Right: A letter from 13-year-old Arioch Wentworth to his father, Bartholomew, written in 1826. A precocious lad, Arioch was already earning his keep as an instructor at boarding schools in southeastern New Hampshire. In the letter at right, Arioch beseeches his father to ferret out more lucrative teaching posts for him. Demonstrating the keen business sense he'd display his whole life, Arioch had recently discovered, to his dismay, that the Madbury school where he was employed had distressingly insufficient funds ("the whole of six dollars and no pence") with which to pay their young instructor.

Arioch signed on with a Boston soapstone supplier in October 1836. He was familiar with the trade, having worked as a quarryman during his teenage summers. Less than six months later, his employer bottomed out during the Great Panic of 1837. Rather than flee to another trade, Arioch made a brave decision. He borrowed money from his father and opened his own soapstone shop on Province Street in Boston. Eight months later, at age 24, he estimated his worth at $1,000. He multiplied these holdings to more than $6 million over the next 65 years of his life.

Mechanical ingenuity and hardnosed business sense had much to do with this success. From 1837 to 1850, soapstone offered Arioch fertile breeding ground for both these talents.

Soapstone is a dense, metamorphic stone with a soft, warm feel. When mined, it has a bluish tone, but with age and oiling it darkens into a rich charcoal gray. In the early 19th century, soapstone was used almost exclusively for fireboxes and hearths because it absorbed heat, released it slowly, and didn't stain or burn.

By the 1840s, however, soapstone had started to be used in the manufacture of other household necessities such as laundry tubs, countertops, and stoves. Arioch was the first to seize on these new opportunities. He quickly developed new methods for fashioning soapstone toward these ends, and built unique machinery to do the job. During the next 13 years, he opened a large manufacturing facility at 19 Hawley Street and increased his wealth 40 times over.

By 1850, soapstone had lost its appeal, not to mention its healthy profit margins, so Arioch sold the operation to his brother, William, and jumped over to the marble business in a small building on Haverhill Street. His timing was impeccable. Boston was on the verge of a building boom; the Commonwealth began to develop what previously had been Massachusetts Bay and marshland into two huge city neighborhoods. The Back Bay and the South End became home to thousands of row houses, brownstones, schools, churches, and institutions. For discerning owners, marble was the material of choice for countless adornments in these new structures. Table tops, bureaus, sideboards, mantels, and fireplaces were some of the appointments that demanded elaborately worked marble.

Arioch Wentworth happened to be the man most able to supply it. From 1850 to 1886, he was the preeminent supplier of marble in the city of Boston. He operated as a classic captain of industry—made all the easier because trustbusting was not yet in vogue. By virtue of his incomparable wealth, Arioch simply bought out any enterprise that threatened his competitive advantage.

Still, resourcefulness and mechanical skill remained the marble supplier's foremost advantages. Much as he had done with soapstone, Arioch invented special machinery to turn out marble in a way that reflected the taste of the times.

"SOME BUSINESS MAXIMS OF ARIOCH WENTWORTH, BOSTON'S SELF-MADE MILLIONAIRE"

- Buy real estate, young man, buy real estate.
- Never fool with a mortgage.
- Always pay 100 cents on the dollar.
- Never pay 100 cents for a dollar.
- Pay all bills when presented.
- Never endorse commercial paper.
- Don't shoulder others' responsibility.
- Work every day till the day's work is done.
- One vacation a year is enough.
- Be sure, then invest—in real estate.
- Lead if you can; follow if you must.
- Leave business at the office.
- Relax the mental tension once a day.
- Reward fealty with fealty.

—Boston Post, March 22, 1903

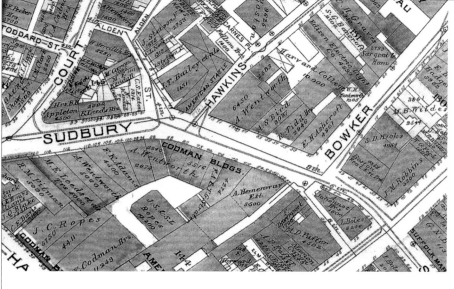

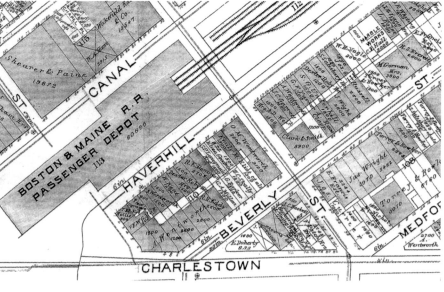

Left: Three 1890 street maps show several of the 50 properties that Arioch Wentworth owned in Boston in the late 19th century.

Above: Very few of Arioch's properties still stand in Boston today. (Most of his holdings were near rail lines. The construction of the Central Artery and North Station demolished the majority of them.) Above are two buildings that remain intact today. Above: 12 Marshall Street, longtime home of the Green Dragon Tavern and neighbor of the oldest dining establishment in the city, the Union Oyster House. Top: 119 High Street in Boston's Financial District.

Arioch Wentworth's Property Holdings (March 1903)

Location	Value
621-623 Atlantic Ave.	$397,900
332 Beacon St. (home)	70,000
16-22 Beverly St.	35,500
88-92 Beverly St.	40,400
73-81 Blackstone St.	84,900
130-145 Blackstone St.	86,000
68 Brimmer St.	48,500
54-58 Broad St.	19,300
19-23 Chardon St.	82,000
102-104 Commercial St.	23,500
114-124 Commercial St.	77,100
170-172 Commercial St.	15,600
198-200 Commercial St.	13,000
223-229 Congress St.	40,000
29-31 Cornhill St.	82,500
117-121 Federal St.	131,900
158-162 Federal St.	64,600
81-103 Friend St.	83,000
104-106 Friend St.	9,000
175 Friend St.	7,000
35 Hartford St.	29,700
13-19 Haverhill St.	41,000
61-63 Haverhill St.	19,500
11-12 Hawkins St.	25,300
119 High St.	57,800
12 Marshall St.	82,500
167-169 Milk St.	28,100
180 North St.	20,900
29-31 Oliver St.	58,000
56-58 Pearl St.	45,700
109-121 Pearl St.	104,900
136-140 Pearl St.	80,800
143 Richmond St.	28,600
59-73 Sudbury St.	219,000
78-100 Sudbury St.	218,200
112-114 Sudbury St.	113,000
27-29 Washington St.	46,000
372 Washington St.	333,000
6-12 Washington St. North	73,000
22-26 Washington St. North	92,000
118 Washington St. North	1,200
23-35 Wendell St.	37,000
Total Assessed Value	**$3,166,900**

Ornate moldings had become the rage and Arioch alone had devised machinery that could cut, polish, and mold marble in large quantities.

Although a ruthless businessman, he was far from a tyrant. Quite the opposite: he actually took unusual interest in his work force. Most of the 300 laborers in his shop had received little schooling; some had received none at all. Arioch, it was said, felt a kinship with his underlings for this reason. Although he had enjoyed an excellent high school education, it was bankrupt of the formal technical training he most desired.

In this discontent the seeds were sown for what would become Wentworth Institute.

Alumnus Eben Bistline, EI&M '34, of Dover, N.H., offers evidence to support the point. His grandfather, Eben Berry, had been a good friend of Arioch Wentworth: "Arioch told my grandfather that he believed young people who earned a living with their hands should have a more formal education in the trade that they chose to follow. He thought there should be a trade school where they could go to learn about it rather than having to work first as a helper, then as an apprentice."

When he finally retired from the marble business in 1886, 73-year-old Arioch Wentworth was quite prosperous. But he soon grew even richer through real estate investments. By the turn of the century, he had grown into the leading land baron in Boston, owning 50 commercial properties. He was no soft touch as a landlord. Tenants often complained to him that they needed elevators in the buildings in order to do business properly. "You may install elevators if you wish," Arioch replied coolly. "At your own expense."

Dedicated Family Man

His later years were, for the most part, happy ones. Arioch had always been a dedicated family man and was especially devoted to his daughter, Susan. He had married Susan Maria Griffiths of Durham, N.H, in 1839. Three years later, their baby son was stillborn—"this loss was always a great grief to him," wrote Arioch's nephew. It made the birth of Susan in November 1845 all the more joyous.

Around 1852, his wife's health began to decline. Because she could no longer keep house, the family boarded in a series of hotels, including many years in a second-story suite at the Tremont House on the corner of Beacon and Tremont Streets. It was there that Arioch's wife died in 1872.

Fortunately, she had enjoyed the pleasure of seeing her daughter's marriage and the birth of her first grandchild. Susan M. Wentworth married Aaron Erickson of Rochester, N.Y., in July 1865. Five years later their son, Arioch Wentworth Erickson, was born. Tragically, the boy's father died the following year in a horrible railroad crash in Revere, Mass., that killed 37 people.

Susan remarried two years later. Her second husband, Willoughby H. Stuart, was British vice consul at Boston. They had a son, Willoughby H. Stuart Jr., in 1874.

The widower Arioch was very close to his daughter and her family. From 1874 on, they lived with him—first in a house he owned at 140 Beacon Street, then in a palatial residence at 332 Beacon Street, which he bought in 1886. They also summered together in a stone mansion at the Mudge Estate in Swampscott, Mass.

In addition to family, he had two overriding passions. The first was horses. On his Swampscott estate, he kept many beautiful trotting horses, including several who "were locally famous," such as Vermont Boy, Lady Planet, and his favorite, a stallion named Gilbreth Knox. His second passion was travel. He had an adventurous spirit and took a trip around the world when he was close to 85 years old. His nephew wrote that Arioch loved travel because "he was always desirous of making acquaintances and talking with people of all degrees."

Arioch Wentworth died of pneumonia on March 12, 1903, in his home at 332 Beacon Street. He was 89 years old.

A PHILANTHROPIST BEYOND COMPARE

His accomplished life notwithstanding, the main reason we remember Arioch Wentworth today is for his posthumous philanthropy. The provisions of the will he drew up in January 1903 defined him as one of the most charitable men of his era. He certainly possessed ample means; Arioch, in fact, ranked in the upper echelon of the 4,000 millionaires who existed in the United States at the turn of the century.

He used this fortune to endow a host of causes, public and private. The largest gift made during his lifetime was $100,000 in 1898 to found the Wentworth Home for the Aged in Dover, N.H., in memory of his parents. He left the home an additional $100,000 in his will. Built a mile west of the farm on which Arioch was raised, the facility remains open to this day; it currently houses 29 elderly women.

Despite having left home for good at age 20, Arioch obviously retained a strong regard for his birthplace. He bequeathed another $100,000 in his will to build the Wentworth Hospital next to the Home for the Aged. Known today as Wentworth-Douglass Hospital, it has thrived for a century as one of the largest medical centers in southern New Hampshire.

The Wentworth Home for the Aged in Dover, N.H. Of the several facilities founded through Arioch's benevolence, the Home for the Aged was the only one built during his lifetime.

Other beneficiaries named in his will were the Society for the Prevention of Cruelty to Animals, the American Humane Educational Society, the Boston YMCA, and Massachusetts Institute of Technology. Each received $100,000. In addition, he gave $10,000 to Bates College in Lewiston, Maine.

Generous as all these bequests were, they accounted, in sum, for only 10 percent of Arioch Wentworth's estate, which was valued at $6.5 million. His intent for the remaining 90 percent was where things truly got interesting.

The grandest of his bequests—the endowment for Wentworth Institute—was valued at $5.4 million.

FAMILY DISCORD

Yet, this extraordinary bequest—and Wentworth Institute—never would have come to pass had not the last year of Arioch Wentworth's life been so melodramatic. The philanthropic legacy that founded Wentworth Institute is tinged with sadness because it arose from a toxic relationship between Arioch Wentworth and his son-in-law.

The family discord sprang from the misdeeds of Willoughby H. Stuart, Susan's husband since 1874 and father of Arioch's second grandson. Despite the prestigious job he held, Stuart's behavior started to unravel in 1899. Friends attributed his mental deterioration to an unusual cause. A Boston Globe newspaper article from March 23, 1903, recounted their story:

"About four years ago, Mr. Stuart had been very badly bitten while trying to separate two bulldogs that were fighting. Both dogs turned on him and Mr. Stuart was fearfully bitten about the arms and body. The shock was said to affect his mind."

Whatever the cause, his state of mind soon led to serious money problems. It was widely known around town that his father-in-law, Arioch Wentworth, had been writing checks for several years to cover Stuart's debts, which were estimated to be at least $115,000. Then, in August 1902, the vice consul's office suddenly dismissed Stuart because of "a peculiar transaction over a note he had signed."

The dismissal, however, did not chasten Mr. Stuart; his plummet continued unabated. A month later, authorities charged him with forging his wife's name to a note for a large amount of money. Susan stood by her husband. She checked him into McLean Asylum in Belmont, Mass., a well-known sanitarium for the well-to-do. (According to newspaper accounts, he was treated for "softening of the brain.")

Throughout the controversy, Stuart's wife, son, and stepson remained devoted to him. His father-in-law, however, did not. Although Arioch Wentworth was a

The front page of the March 24, 1903, Boston Post tabloid. Each of the city's newspapers (which were plentiful at the turn of the century) eagerly covered the events relating to Arioch's death and the dramatic revelations contained in his last will and testament. Willoughby Stuart is depicted in the inset at top right. Arioch's 332 Beacon Street home is shown in the bottom inset.

sentimental family man, he was just as much a coldblooded businessman. A mere four months after Willoughby Stuart's misadventures came to light, Arioch Wentworth rewrote the will he had first drafted in 1887. The bulk of his fortune, which previously would have landed in the hands of his daughter and grandchildren, was now directed toward other philanthropic ends. It boiled down to one fact: Arioch Wentworth did not want his hard-earned millions swallowed up by the known and unknown debts amassed by his son-in-law.

The last few months of Arioch's life were sad ones. He and his daughter remained close; she and the children lived at his house until he died on March 12, 1903. But they were each wounded by the conflict over Willoughby Stuart.

The tension erupted 11 days after Arioch Wentworth died, at the reading of his will on March 23, 1903.

A CONTROVERSIAL CODICIL

Arioch Wentworth's will had been executed on January 22, 1903, two months before he died. The first three parts of the will detailed bequests to his sisters, nephews, and nieces, as well as his clerk. Parts four through ten outlined various charitable contributions ranging from $10,000 to $100,000. Part eleven was the real eye-opener.

Here, Arioch charged that the remainder of his property ($5.4 million worth) be held in trust. He named four men as trustees, including his lawyer, Paul Barron Watson, who had drawn the will for him. The fifth trustee was his daughter, Susan. Next came the 36 words [*see Page 3*] that announced his desire to found Wentworth Institute.

As for distributing his fortune, here's how he envisioned it: A fixed portion of the net income from the trust was to be distributed quarterly each year to Arioch's daughter and two grandsons. The sums he chose were surprisingly small. To Susan he intended to bestow $3,000 each quarter for the remainder of her life. (She was 58 years old at the time he died.) Arioch W. Erickson and Willoughby H. Stuart Jr. would each receive $2,000 per quarter for the remainder of their respective lives. In addition, Erickson's wife, Cecile, was due $1,000 each quarter. The rest of the net income each year, instructed Arioch, was to fund the operation of Wentworth Institute.

It was a curious decision by Arioch. With an estate as rich as his, he surely realized that Wentworth Institute would end up receiving at least eight times more income from the trust each year than would his family members combined.

But while this may have been his last will and testament, it was, of course, not his first. This was the crux of Susan Stuart's argument when she opposed the probate of her father's 1903 will.

Less than a month after her father was buried, Susan furnished evidence to the probate court for Essex County that "said Arioch Wentworth executed another instrument purporting to be a will, dated October 6, 1887." The contents of this will were not the least bit similar to the 1903 will. For one thing, the 1887 will directed practically all of Arioch's financial benevolence toward his family. The only public bequests it set forth were $100,000 to establish a "Wentworth Wing" in the Boston Museum of Fine Arts, then located on Dartmouth Street, and $100,000 to build a library for the town of Rollinsford, N.H. The remainder of Arioch's holdings was to be divided among his daughter and grandsons. No mention was made of Wentworth Institute, Susan pointed out.

Furthermore, she claimed that her father was not of sound mind when he wrote the 1903 codicil.

But the Institute had long been on Arioch's mind, countered his lawyer and confidant, Paul Watson. "Arioch Wentworth cherished the belief that all big things in this world were made with human hands," he wrote. "He resolved to establish a school for mechanics, and he used to boast that some day Wentworth Institute would prove of greater value than any school which sought to teach its students solely by the use of books."

After nine months of hearings in probate court, a mediator negotiated a compromise on Christmas Eve, 1903. It set forth a 50-50 split. Half of Arioch's $5.4 million fortune went to Susan Stuart to distribute equally among the heirs. The other half transferred to the trustees named by Arioch for organizing a corporation known as Wentworth Institute.

1904

1911

The Founding Era, 1904-1911

Arioch Wentworth entrusted five people with the duty of carrying out his wishes to found a school of mechanical arts. Two soon dropped out, leaving three loyalists as the founding directors: Paul B. Watson, who had been Arioch's lawyer; Frederic Atherton, an old business acquaintance of Arioch; and William H. Wentworth, his most beloved nephew. These trustees quickly recruited four other talented individuals to join their group, including John Davis Long, a former governor and U.S. congressman, and George Wigglesworth, a topflight attorney. Joshua M. Sears and another nephew, Oliver M. Wentworth, rounded out the crew.

The first step for these seven directors was to establish a corporation under the laws of the Commonwealth of Massachusetts. It was a fairly easy task, considering the outstanding connections these seven men had fostered in their lifetimes. The most politically wired member, John Davis Long, became chairman of the board, and the most passionate and devoted member, Paul Watson, was named treasurer. In less than four months, on April 5, 1904, a charter was granted to establish a corporation under the name of Wentworth Institute.

Top left: Paul Barron Watson, a Harvard-educated lawyer, was Arioch Wentworth's counsel and friend. After Arioch's death in 1903, Watson spent the next 45 years as the steward of his friend's greatest dream. From 1904 to 1948, he was treasurer of Wentworth Institute and the most influential of the school's directors.

Left: A 1911 photograph of the first two facilities built by the directors of Wentworth Institute. The Power Plant, left, was completed in 1910. Next came the West Building, right, whose appearance and function merged the sensibilities of a school and a factory.

Below: A 1914 view from what is today Wentworth's West Parking Lot. The foundry wing is at far left.

```
No. 10335
                    COMMONWEALTH OF MASSACHUSETTS

BE IT KNOWN That whereas John D. Long, Paul Barron Watson, Joshua M.
Sears, William H. Wentworth, Frederick Atherton, George Wigglesworth and
Oliver M. Wentworth

have associated themselves with the intention of forming a corporation
under the name of the                    Wentworth Institute,

for the purpose of furnishing education in the mechanical arts,


and have complied with the provisions of the statutes of the Commonwealth
in such case made and provided, as appears from the certificate of the
                    President, Treasurer, and Directors
of said corporation, duly approved by the Commissioner of Corporations
and recorded in this office:
    NOW, THEREFORE, I, WILLIAM M. OLIN, Secretary of the Commonwealth
of Massachusetts, DO HEREBY CERTIFY that said
John D. Long, Paul Barron Watson, Joshua M. Sears, William H. Wentworth,
Frederick Atherton, George Wigglesworth and Oliver M. Wentworth,
their associates and successors, are legally organized and established as,
and are hereby made, an existing corporation under the name of the
                    Wentworth Institute,
with the powers, rights and privileges, and subject to the limitations,
duties and restrictions, which by law appertain thereto.
                    WITNESS my official signature hereunto subscribed,
                    and the Great Seal of the Commonwealth of
                    Massachusetts hereunto affixed, this
                    fifth day of April in the year of our Lord
       (SEAL)       one thousand nine hundred and four
                         (Signed)  Wm. M. Olin
                                   Secretary of the Commonwealth.
    I hereby certify that the foregoing is a correct copy of the Charter
of Wentworth Institute.
                         (Signed)   Paul Barron Watson
```

Above: The Institute's first director of the board, John Davis Long, was a career politician with an impeccable pedigree.

Left: On April 5, 1904, charter number 10335 certified Wentworth Institute as a corporation in the Commonwealth of Massachusetts.

Although the directors had acted quickly in forging a charter, they moved more deliberately in other matters. The groundbreaking for the first campus building, for instance, did not occur until October 1910. Two reasons explain this six-and-a-half-year delay.

For one, treasurer Paul Watson was a shrewd, conservative manager of the bequest that Arioch Wentworth had endowed to found the school. Watson carefully resisted dipping into the endowment's principal during those early years. As a result, by 1910 the endowment had accrued more than $850,000 in interest—enough money for the treasurer to fund both capital and operational expenses for the new Institute.

The second reason was that the directors needed time to research and define the mission and strategy of the new institution. ("Steering our bark over uncharted seas," was how the literate Watson referred to the task.)

Arioch Wentworth, of course, had laid out a succinct mission for the school in his will. His words were, "for the purpose of furnishing education in the mechanical arts." But such a mission, although marvelously direct, demanded considerable interpretation.

That's where the directors came in. "Mechanical arts" held a very specific meaning to them. It indicated that instruction should center on trades relating to wood and metal. Moreover, the very specificity of that phrase, "mechanical arts," suggested to the directors that Arioch Wentworth did not envision this school as a rival of upper-tier science and engineering schools such as Massachusetts Institute of Technology or Stevens Institute of Technology in Hoboken, New Jersey. Rather, they inferred, the founder intended Wentworth Institute to be more vocational in nature, a training place where young men could gain proficiency in a skilled trade.

But that left the directors with few precedents to follow. As Watson wrote, "Trade schools did not exist in this community, and the only examples to guide us in our endeavor were undeveloped institutions in other states and a few schools operated by foreign governments under conditions hardly applicable here. So if we were to avoid the pitfalls that threaten every new institution, we needed to proceed with utmost care."

They did just that. In one respect, the seven directors were an unusual assemblage of talent to be given the job of building a trade school from the ground up. They were, unquestionably, well-educated and highly accomplished men: ex-governors, lawyers, judges. For the most part, however, these were also men whose hands had never borne calluses, whose nicely tailored clothing had never been streaked with grease or coated with sawdust.

The Honorable Robert Grant was one of these directors; he served on the board from 1905 to 1921. He later wrote, "I remember wondering why I was thought suitable for the service and I hesitated about accepting, for I was so steeped in law and literature as to be literally an ignoramus on the mechanical arts. I still have to think for a moment before I am sure whether the sun revolves around the earth or the earth round the sun. What led me to accept was my warm friendship and admiration for Governor Long and George Wigglesworth, who were wise and efficient in their generation and who knew only a little more about science than I."

Though they may not have been mechanically inclined, the directors were wise and deliberate. They spent six years listening to the counsel of experts and refining their plans for Wentworth Institute.

AT THE TIME THE DIRECTORS PURCHASED THE LAND FOR THE WENTWORTH CAMPUS IN 1908, THE NEIGHBORHOOD WAS BEST KNOWN AS THE LOCALE OF THE HUNTINGTON AVENUE GROUNDS, HOME OF THE BOSTON RED SOX FROM 1901 UNTIL 1912, WHEN FENWAY PARK OPENED. TODAY, NORTHEASTERN UNIVERSITY'S CABOT GYMNASIUM RESIDES ON THE SITE OF THE FORMER BALL GROUNDS.

A School for "Serious-Minded Boys"

An important challenge for the directors was to define a target audience. One stark fact jumped out at them: at the time, only one out of eight boys in the United States entered adulthood with more than an eighth-grade education.

That one out of eight, the directors reasoned, surely would be uninterested in Wentworth Institute's offerings. But it was the 88 percent majority—the undereducated seven out of eight young men—where opportunity beckoned. The directors sketched out the prospects for such individuals:

"Two courses are open to the young man whose studies stopped at the grammar school period, and who asks himself in all seriousness what he is going to do for a living. He must either follow in the footsteps of his father or grandfather, if they were carpenters, builders, or mechanics, and apprentice himself to some neighbor as an errand boy in a shop, or he will make a systematic study of the opportunities of trade school education and in a practical and businesslike way, lay the foundation for his career."

The first path, apprenticeship, was a time-honored, respected tradition in the trades but lately had grown as noteworthy for its hardships and handicaps as for its benefits. The directors, therefore, seized upon the second path as the beacon for Wentworth Institute.

Among this undereducated majority, they singled out two general types of people as tailor-made for a Wentworth education. One was the young man, say 16 years old, who saw himself working down the line as a mechanic, electrician, or plumber. The directors would say to this person, "Son, although nothing can take the place of practical experience working at your trade, what Wentworth Institute can do is materially shorten the time required for you to lay a solid foundation. So when you do come into contact with the work you desire, your advancement will be more rapid than you possibly could have secured under the methods of apprenticeship."

The second type was the slightly older man, say 22 years old, who already had four or five years of work under his belt. To this individual, the directors would say, "Sir, you've proven yourself a worthy practitioner in your factory (shop, mill, etc.). But you're probably discouraged with the lack of progress you're making. There's a cure for this dead end. Enroll at Wentworth Institute—you can even attend night classes—and our systematized methods of instruction will soon have you ready to fill a position as a foreman or superintendent."

These two types of likely applicants guided the way in which the Institute packaged its offerings. The directors geared one-year day courses for the young man as yet unexposed to any specialized line of work. These programs built general core competencies and offered a sort of "crash-course" immersion in introductory skills relating to a specific trade, such as carpentry or plumbing.

Two-year courses, on the other hand, were pitched at the experienced worker who wished to ascend to the next level in his field. A two-year course, taken at day or night, enabled students to gain more practical shop experience, and also to supplement instruction in related trades. With this expansion of skills and perspective, a graduate was well-positioned for advancement in his profession.

As they investigated the direction Wentworth Institute should take, the directors put great stock in research conducted by James Dodge, a Philadelphia-based manufacturer of coal machinery and president of the American Society of Mechanical Engineers. In 1908, Dodge presented data that set forth the economic argument for Wentworth's potential usefulness to young men.

According to Dodge's report, an untrained man reached his maximum earning power ($10.20 a week) at 22 years of age. The average apprentice started at a wage of $5 a week at age 16, jumped to $9 a week four years later, rose to $13.50 a week at age 22, and maxed out at age 24 earning $15.80 a week. In contrast to these scenarios was the boy who spent the years from 16 to 19 "studying and practicing in a reliable trade school." This educated worker could expect an average wage of $12 a week right out of school, $18 a week at age 23, and $22 a week at age 25—a 40 percent improvement over his apprentice-trained brethren and a 116 percent leap over the untrained laborer.

Having pored over this report, the directors of Wentworth Institute wrote this conclusion: "Between 16 and 19 are the precious years in a boy's life. It is to serious-minded boys of these ages that Wentworth Institute makes its appeal."

The next decision for the directors was to hash out exactly which "mechanical arts" the school would teach. To accomplish this, the directors set off to learn what the marketplace was demanding. They arranged meetings with industrialists such as mill owners and electrical contractors, and trade societies such as the Central Labor Union and the American Society of Mechanical Engineers. After securing this data, the directors considered the important question, "What can we *afford* to teach?" The result was a curriculum [*see 1911–12 Catalog excerpt on Pages 20-21*] consisting of a dozen programs that the Institute could teach affordably and well, and that would satisfy a need in the working world.

WENTWORTH INSTITUTE WAS ONE OF TWO POSTSECONDARY SCHOOLS FOUNDED IN THE COMMONWEALTH OF MASSACHUSETTS IN 1904. THE OTHER WAS ASSUMPTION COLLEGE IN WORCESTER.

Life might have been easier for the directors had they modeled their school after an existing institution of similar purpose. In 1911, there were about a dozen industrial day schools in Massachusetts, the two largest being the New Bedford Industrial School (202 students) and the Worcester Trade School (180 students). The directors, however, emphatically chose a more rigorous approach, as they wrote in a 1911 report: "Our new Institute is carefully avoiding duplica-

A SUMMARY OF THE CURRICULAR OFFERINGS DURING
WENTWORTH INSTITUTE'S FIRST YEAR

ONE-YEAR DAY COURSES
*Intended for beginners and persons who have had little
practical experience*

Carpentry and Building: Shop practice includes joinery, roof framing, stair building, wood turning, and mill work. A lot of time spent as well on reading plans and blueprints.

Electric Wiring: "The surprisingly rapid development of the electrical industries and the increasing number and variety of electric appliances that are coming into general use give to this trade an assurance of continued growth." Special emphasis is given to the scientific principles of electricity and magnetism.

Foundry Practice: "Perhaps no branch of manufacturing has been more neglected in recent years, and in none is there greater opportunity for distinct advancement through the application of scientific principles and economies in methods of manufacture." Shop experience includes using different kinds of sand, making cores by hand, and lining, charging, and managing the cupola.

Machine Work: "No trade, it is believed, offers more excellent or a greater variety of opportunities to the young man. The United States is more and more becoming a manufacturing country, dependent upon the machine trade; and New England especially is the center of machine-trade industries that are growing steadily toward the finer and higher grades of work." This program "cannot turn out finished workmen, but it is expected that its graduates will be advanced apprentices with good earning power at the time of graduation." Plenty of experience in operating the principal machine shop tools, such as the shaper, planer, engine lathe, drill press, and milling machine. Later comes work with grinders and boring mills.

Pattern Making: "The pattern maker is the first person to give definite form to new designs of machinery, a trade of much importance in modern industry." But it is a trade in which apprenticeship has disappeared, therefore leaving the trade school as the sole venue of instruction. Instructors offer practical demonstrations "of the way in which patterns are molded in sand, the way in which cores are set, and castings made and finished, in order that students may better understand the problems in drafts, shrinkage, size and location of fillets, parting, etc., that are continually arising in the trade."

Plumbing: "The health of the community is closely dependent upon sanitary plumbing, and the efficient journeyman plumber should be not only skillful in the execution of his work, but also should have a thorough comprehension of those fundamental principles of sanitation that are essential." The average wages of the skilled journeyman plumber were $32.25 per week—a number that "greatly exceeds the salary paid to clerks, bookkeepers, and stenographers of equal experience."

TWO-YEAR DAY COURSES

Intended for those who wish to become superior workmen, master mechanics, foremen, etc.

Architectural Construction: Geared toward young men who wish to become foremen or superintendents in the building industry, this program emphasizes practical construction methods while at the same time giving ample instruction in theory and design so as to enable the student to appreciate the structural and artistic features of the architect's work.

Electrical Construction and Operation: Practical work in the laboratory includes "experience in operating and repairing, and practice in connecting and making ready for service, the many types of modern generators, motors, rotary converters, transformers, engines and auxiliary apparatus, and instruments with which the school is equipped."

Foundry Management and Operation: "All sorts of castings of iron, steel, aluminum, brass, and bronze are required in the manufacture of machinery. The foundryman is required to produce these castings on a large scale, absolutely uniform in quality, with finish of a high grade, and at the lowest possible cost." Despite a strong trend in the trade toward specialization, the Institute's instruction emphasizes versatility.

Machine Construction and Tool Design: This course is "intended to train young men for the higher grades of work in such industries as the manufacture of machine tools, steam and gas engines, steam pumps, automobiles, shoe machinery, cotton machinery, conveying apparatus, automatic machinery, tools and builders' hardware, and the manufacture of a large number of similar articles made from iron, steel, and brass."

EVENING COURSES

Intended for those who are employed during the daytime

The evening curriculum features many of the same courses as daytime, as well as:

- **Practical Mechanics;**
- **Strength and Properties of Materials;**
- **Reinforced Concrete and Fireproof Building Construction;**
- **Steam Engine and the Operation of Power Plants; and**
- **Electrical Machinery (alternate current & direct current).**

THREE IMPORTANT NOTES

- Applicants for admission must be thoroughly in earnest.
- For all courses, half the time is spent in shop practice; the other half is spent in practical mechanics, practical mathematics, and topics such as drafting and blueprint reading.
- Tuition: $6 per term.

Photos, from left:

1916 carpentry and building students learn to frame a house.

1913 electric wiring class, led by Wallace Mayo (leaning against wall). The students are learning a method called "open" or "cleat" wiring.

Evening students work in the motor lab, 1913.

Pattern making shop, 1912.

tion of any existing educational opportunities. It seeks not to supplant existing schools. As a matter of fact, it occupies a field not touched by any, although in certain instances they may teach certain subjects called by the same name; but where they do so, they teach them to young men who will use them for a totally different purpose."

True to the founder's charitable intent, the directors set up Wentworth Institute to be decidedly not-for-profit. In a decision enabled by Arioch Wentworth's huge endowment, tuition for the first class in 1911 was set at a measly $6 per term ($18 per year). That was small money, even in 1911 dollars. "If we were to charge a tuition fee sufficient to cover the cost of instructors," wrote the directors, "it would frustrate the plans of the school for teaching working boys or men in smaller positions." In fact, the directors strongly considered charging no tuition at all, but ultimately decided to charge just enough money to prevent unmotivated pupils from applying.

Location, Location, Location

At the same time the directors were figuring out whom and what would be taught, they were engaged in the search for where the teaching would take place. The directors shopped patiently for land. It needed to be in the city, first of all. In an era when most transportation happened on rail lines, accessibility was a high priority. Moreover, the city offered proximity to the industries for which Wentworth would be graduating skilled labor.

After a four-and-a-half-year wait, the trustees found their opportunity in 1908. Owners of a large plot of land in the shadow of Mission Hill, the Sewall & Day Cordage Company had operated in Roxbury since 1834. The company made rope for clipper ships. Up until the late 19th century, a long canal bordered the west side of Parker Street in the Mission Hill district. A mill had operated there since 1658, taking advantage of the location where the Stony Brook emptied into a tidal basin. It was here that Sewall & Day built a complex of ropewalks, ten storehouses, a carpet shop, stables, a mill, a tar house, boiler house, and offices. The heart of their operation was the corner of Parker and Ruggles Streets. In 1873, the company employed more than 300 people.

By the late 1800s, however, Boston's development conspired against Sewall & Day's Roxbury location. In the 1850s, city planners filled in Back Bay and culverted Stony Brook. As a result, Sewall & Day lost access to its most precious resource, water. The company moved its operations to Allston in the 1890s and, after several years, placed its Roxbury property on the market.

In 1908, Sewall & Day and Wentworth Institute found each other. Wentworth's directors liked the look of the property; it was 13 acres of land in an appealing locale. The Museum of Fine Arts was being constructed across Huntington Avenue, after years of having resided in Copley Square. Several colleges had

PLATE 36.

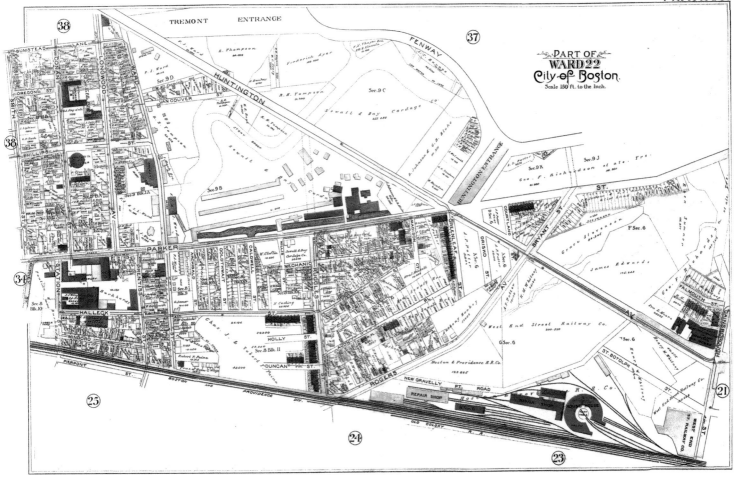

Above: Horsepower of a literal sort supplied the resources that constructed the 38,000-square-foot West Building in 1910-11.

Top: An 1890 map of Boston's Ward 22, which became home to Wentworth Institute in 1908. Sewall & Day Cordage Company's ropewalks (Section 9B on the map) dominated the landscape north of Parker Street. Sewall & Day's operations were powered by the Stony Brook until city planners culverted the waterway. To this day, Wentworth's property line bisects Stony Brook's sinuous path.

recently arrived in the neighborhood. The medical schools of Harvard and Tufts were nearby on Longwood Avenue, Simmons College had opened eight years earlier, and the Boston Normal School (today Massachusetts College of Art) was a stone's throw away. Sealing the deal was the presence of numerous factories and industrial concerns (breweries were especially common) within a mile of the Sewall & Day lot.

On November 17, 1908, the directors completed the purchase. It cost them $446,500. The deed consisted of two tracts of land. A 359,000-square-foot lot bounded by Huntington, Ruggles, Parker, and Ward streets previously housed an odd mix of service buildings for Sewall & Day. A smaller, triangular lot (140,000 square feet) across from the brand-new museum on Huntington Avenue, had been for years an unsightly pit that Sewall & Day filled with water in the winter and ran as an outdoor skating rink.

As befits a school specializing in mechanical and industrial arts, the first facility the directors built was the Power Plant. Completed in 1910, it was the first of four buildings that Boston architects Peabody & Stearns designed for Wentworth Institute over a six-year period. One hundred years later, their academic

Numbers Through the Years			
Year	Enrollment*	Graduates*	Tuition
1911–12	244	91	$18
1912–13	341	155	
1913–14	363	186	
1914–15	482	202	
1915–16	517	255	
1916–17	626	254	
1917–18	598	207	
1918–19	383	155	
1919–20	625	275	
1920–21	605	274	$45
1921–22	652	307	
1922–23	636	300	
1923–24	567	305	
1924–25	618	324	
1925–26	654	355	
1926–27	675	359	
1927–28	681	393	
1928–29	659	398	$125
1929–30	639	361	
1930–31	692	354	
1931–32	699	343	
1932–33	546	244	
1933–34	458	176	
1934–35	492	187	
1935–36	507	164	
1936–37	581	211	
1937–38	609	219	
1938–39	596	261	
1939–40	576	248	$175
1940–41	602	254	
1941–42	533	265	
1942–43	348	150	
1943–44**	0	0	
1944–45	0	0	
1945–46	113	29	
1946–47	364	168	
1947–48	583	357	
1948–49	540	302	
1949–50	611	346	
1950–51	592	340	
1951–52	526	270	
1952–53	569	190	$400
1953–54	607	189	
1954–55	745	238	
1955–56	921	314	
1956–57	1056	316	
1957–58	1249	383	
1958–59	1399	341	
1959–60	1502	375	
1960–61	1795	475	
1961–62	1962	572	
1962–63	1966	606	
1963–64	2080	613	$720
1964–65	2196	611	
1965–66	2374	852	
1966–67	2241	874	
1967–68	2031	815	
1968–69	2017	804	
1969–70	1845	742	
1970–71	1805	602	
1971–72	1724	714	
1972–73	1765	729	
1973–74	1803	646	
1974–75	1681	624	
1975–76	1876	565	
1976–77	2008	680	
1977–78	2078	641	
1978–79	2042	640	$2,450
1979–80	2501	691	
1980–81	2772	862	
1981–82	3026	912	
1982–83	3282	1082	
1983–84	3321	1036	
1984–85	3245	985	
1985–86	3258	971	
1986–87	3180	930	
1987–88	2834	944	
1988–89	2962	905	
1989–90	3034	953	$6,870
1990–91	2904	1033	
1991–92	2734	1031	
1992–93	2603	839	
1993–94	2389	866	
1994–95	2232	682	
1995–96	2116	638	
1996–97	2288	537	
1997–98	2487	526	
1998–99	2494	457	
1999–2000	2661	520	
2000–01	2658	568	
2001–02	2765	627	
2002–03	2823	727	
2003–04	2850	—	$15,000

complex (known today as Williston Hall, Wentworth Hall, and Dobbs Hall) remains the defining facade of Wentworth Institute of Technology.

The second building, the construction of which started in 1910, was a five-story structure called the Shop Building or the West Building (today it is Williston Hall). The foundry occupied a wing of the 145-by-49-foot building; the West Building itself included a carpenter shop, pattern shop, machine shop, blacksmith shop, plumbing shop, and electric wiring room. A small wing contained administrative offices. The building was completed in September 1911.

It cost $250,000 to construct these first two buildings.

The final item on the director's punchlist was to hire a principal to lead the newborn Institute. Their first choice, Arthur L. Williston of Pratt Institute, accepted the offer in 1910 and arrived in Boston to take charge.

The directors had accomplished a great deal in seven-and-a-half years. The endowment had grown substantially, an excellent location had been secured, a campus had begun to take shape, a one-sentence mission statement had been fleshed out into a real curriculum, and perhaps the best available candidate in the entire country had been hired to run the school.

Now, all Wentworth Institute needed was students. They arrived, dressed to the nines, at 8:00 a.m. on Monday, September 25, 1911.

*Numbers apply to day students only.

**Wentworth closed from May 1943 to January 1946 to focus on its wartime duties as a training center for Navy personnel.

From 1910 to 1916, construction was a constant presence on the Wentworth campus. Here, scaffolding shrouds the half-finished East Building (Dobbs Hall) in 1916. Once completed, the facility housed building laboratories and a strength of materials lab on the basement level, a carpentry shop and drafting room on the first floor, and the printing program on the upper levels. Today, 88 years after the hall opened, the strength of materials lab continues to occupy the basement level.

1. Arioch Wentworth
The Founder

Without dispute, the most important man in the history of Wentworth Institute of Technology is Wentworth himself. The Institute exists today for one simple reason: because Arioch Wentworth desired to create a school that would "furnish education in the mechanical arts." Surely, the idea for such an institution lived a long time inside his head, yet he did not write it on paper until seven weeks before he died on March 12, 1903. Whether or not the 89-year-old man was thinking clearly at the time ultimately turned out to be a $2.7 million question. But 100 years later, the argument is irrelevant. What is relevant is the fact that he was thinking wisely. His brainchild has flourished for a full century, has produced nearly 40,000 graduates, and enters its second century poised to build on the successes of its first.

2. John Davis Long
The Statesman

Starting a school from scratch is tricky business. Wentworth's Institute's first chairman of the board, John Davis Long, was one of only a few men at the time capable of the job. An extraordinary political career qualified him to guide the brand-new Institute. His record as a statesman stands as one of the most accomplished in Massachusetts annals. He was speaker of the state house of representatives from 1875 to 1878, governor from 1880 to 1882, a three-term U.S. Congressman, and U.S. Secretary of the Navy from 1897 to 1902. A year later, he brokered the resolution of Arioch Wentworth's estate, mediating a compromise between Arioch's daughter, Susan, and the assigned directors of Wentworth Institute. In 1904, these same directors recruited Long to head Wentworth's board, a task he carried out skillfully until his death in 1915.

3. Paul B. Watson
The Guardian

No one influenced Wentworth Institute's first four decades more than Paul Barron Watson. As Arioch Wentworth's personal lawyer, he drew up the founder's famous 1903 will. In the will, Arioch named Watson one of the five founding directors of the Institute. As treasurer, he took immediate charge of the Institute's finances. A savvy money manager, he kept the Institute on firm financial footing, helping the school prosper despite two World Wars and a Great Depression. His influence, however, extended far beyond dollars and cents. During his 44 years on the board, Watson was the man to whom both principals and fellow directors deferred. From his office at 20 State Street in Boston, he maintained a daily correspondence with Wentworth's first two principals, Arthur Williston and Frederick Dobbs. In pristinely hand-written letters, Mr. Watson advised on topics both

mundane and essential: from how deep to dig fence posts for the front gate, to when the Institute should consign an academic program to the ash heap. The Harvard-educated Watson was a renaissance man who favored history and philosophy. He wrote a number of books in his lifetime, including two before he turned 30: *The Swedish Revolution Under Gustavus Vasa* and *Marcus Aurelius Antoninus*. He was a man of many professional accomplishments, none more remarkable than his splendid stewardship of Wentworth Institute.

4. William H. Wentworth
The Historian

Much of what we know about the founder of Wentworth Institute comes courtesy of a brief biography written in 1913 by his favorite nephew, William Hall Wentworth. William's father, also named William, had acquired his brother Arioch's Boston-based soapstone business in 1850. William the younger inherited the business and maintained close ties with his uncle. Arioch named him a founding director of Wentworth Institute in his will. A resident of Lexington, Mass., William served on the Institute's board of directors from 1904 until his death in 1935. His son Reginald also served on the board for many years. William prefaced the historical sketch of his uncle with these words: "I have given some details which will be of little interest to those of the present day, but it may be that the lapse of time and the growth of Wentworth Institute may arouse more interest in the founder." How true.

The Museum of Fine Arts opened its Huntington Avenue facility in 1909. One of the MFA's most beloved landmarks is the "Appeal to the Great Spirit" statue (*above*) on the front lawn. Its sculptor, Cyrus Dallin, also designed the World War II plaque (*below*) that hangs outside Wentworth's Watson Auditorium.

1911

1923

The Williston Era, 1911-1923

A school begun badly is a school doomed for failure. The directors of Wentworth Institute found the man they wanted to ensure that their school wouldn't fall prey to that fate.

Arthur Lyman Williston had been for 12 years the director of the School of Science and Technology at Pratt Institute in Brooklyn, N.Y. This was no small matter, as Pratt was the closest thing Wentworth had for a role model. Following a three-year study of similar institutions in Europe, Pratt had been founded in 1887 as an institution where pupils "could learn trades through skillful use of their hands." By 1910, it was considered the country's leading school for industrial training. Because Williston had contributed much to that school's successful development, Wentworth Institute's directors regarded him as a man ready and able to catch lightning in a bottle a second time.

They figured right. With a mixture of gentlemanly manners and a passion for order and organization, Williston made Wentworth Institute immediately viable. He molded the Institute in a style that remains its trademark to this day. Whereas a sort of arty, bohemian spirit defined Pratt Institute, Wentworth quickly adopted the personality of its first principal. The Institute was no-nonsense; rules mattered, discipline was religion. Laboratories were kept clean and orderly; attendance was closely monitored. Courses of study were demanding and rigidly defined.

Top Left: Arthur Lyman Williston, Wentworth Institute's first principal.

Left: Under the direction of young instructor George Tapp, MW '13, machine construction and tool design students from the Class of 1914 "heat it up" in the West Building's forge shop.

Below: During the first week of classes in September 1911, Institute instructors set students to work installing a shaft-governed engine made by the Brown Company.

Williston eagerly imbued his institution, faculty, and students with a sense of purpose. From day one, he sternly preached the gospel of Wentworth as a school with its sleeves rolled up and its feet set firmly on the ground. It was a school that filled a need. Schools such as Harvard University and Massachusetts Institute of Technology produced engineers and architects. But the ideas and plans of their graduates would remain forever unfulfilled if not for intelligent implementation performed by skilled technicians. Williston targeted this second tier of the engineering trades as the niche for Wentworth Institute.

Hands On

Arthur Williston not only coined the term, "technical institute," he also pioneered the hands-on approach to running such a school.

From the beginning, "hands-on" was a defining characteristic of Wentworth Institute. As Principal Williston wrote in the first catalog, "The board of directors of Wentworth Institute adheres strictly to the plan of the founder to furnish education in the mechanical arts. The purpose is to train young men for efficiency in skilled trades. The instruction, therefore, is designed to cultivate intelligence as well as manual skill and dexterity."

Above: The steam laboratory in the Power Plant served two masters. In addition to generating power for Institute facilities, it was also a proving ground for evening students in the steam engine and power practice program.

Right: Students install a locomotive boiler in 1914. Pupils at the time joked that they were nothing more than cheap labor for Principal Williston to exploit.

Machine construction and tool design students stoke the steam boiler in 1914. While instructors taught students every hands-on trick in the trade, they were less successful in imparting common sense lessons such as, "Don't wear a white dress shirt on the day you're working on boilers."

Every aspect of Wentworth Institute supported the "hands-on" mission. Williston liked to point out, for example, that the Institute's Power Plant not only kept the school's lights on, but also acted as a working laboratory for Wentworth students. Study of the operation and testing of steam and gas engines and boilers, and electric generators and motors all took place in the Power Plant. And not on retread or hand-me-down equipment, but on the finest boilers, generators, and engines available at the time. "Instruction in the principles," Williston boasted, "is given not upon specially designed or peculiar apparatus but, in every instance, upon the very machinery which the students will later be required to handle or operate as expert mechanics."

Williston's leadership style embodied the hands-on theme. His enthusiasm was infectious. A mere two weeks after taking over as principal in 1910, he mailed thousands of letters to high school principals and captains of industry, trumpeting Wentworth's offerings. "This is both the latest and the most extensive development in trade teaching and industrial education anywhere in the United States," he wrote.

Nevertheless, plenty of challenges loomed for the principal in 1910. The two most pressing were to assemble a competent faculty and to oversee development of the campus master plan.

A School Is Only as Strong as Its Faculty

Finding qualified instructors was difficult. The principal enjoyed few opportunities to lure experienced teachers from similar schools, because such institutions were few and far between. So instead, Williston knocked on the doors of industry to fill Wentworth Institute's faculty ranks.

John Mickelson, who taught pattern making and machine design at Wentworth Institute for 30 years.

One of the first faculty members he hired was John Mickelson, whom he named the head of the Pattern Making Department. Mickelson represented the gold standard of Wentworth instructors—a seasoned professional who possessed not only a wealth of practical experience, but also a zeal for transferring his encyclopedic knowledge to the next generation of qualified workers. He had been head pattern maker for the Allis-Chambers Company, where he designed some of the working patterns used in the construction of Niagara Falls' power plant equipment. He also designed and built one of the first four-cylinder automotive gasoline engines, which the Stutz Motor Company subsequently purchased.

A 1912 Boston Transcript newspaper article commended the new Institute's industry-hardened faculty: "Their teachers combine practical training with pedagogical training. There is not a man at the head of a department in the Institute who has not been a journeyman in his trade, and is therefore a practical man who thoroughly understands working conditions and is teaching practical knowledge."

A faculty force such as this cemented forever the Institute's hands-on philosophy. This would never be an "ivory tower" institution. Instructors who came fresh from the front lines of industry (and most of whom continued to work at their original jobs during the Institute's summer breaks) instilled at Wentworth a culture of learning that remains very much in place to this day. The instructors taught students a trade in much the same way they used to bring new recruits in the workplace up to speed. Which is to say, practice invariably took precedence over theory. Yes, the underlying theory would be taught for any given situation. (Wentworth had, after all, promised to teach its students "how to think.") But as soon as that groundwork was established, the bulk of the teaching took place not on the blackboard, but in the shop or laboratory.

The first faculty of Wentworth Institute. Arthur Williston is seated, fourth from left. Wentworth's second principal, Frederick Dobbs, is seated, second from right.

This philosophy revealed itself in the way Williston crafted the Institute's mathematics instruction. For one thing, he insisted on naming the department, "Practical Mathematics." And the teaching certainly reflected this name. Algebraic theorems and differential equations remained largely unexplored terrain at Wentworth Institute. Instead, applications got top billing. Consider, for instance, the curriculum as it applied to a carpentry and building student. Williston considered math useful for him only so far as it aided in "estimating quantities of material from architects' plans and specifications and, in addition to this, making out bills of materials for work done in the shop, with proper allowances for finish, waste, etc." Williston liked to point out that carpenters in the apprentice system were trained only to give rough estimates of what a certain piece of work might cost. By contrast, a Wentworth-educated carpenter had a professional advantage. "No man," warned the principal, "can afford to guess what his profits are going to be or take chances with a piece of first-class woodwork."

By September 1911, Williston had assembled a faculty of 19 capable men. They included Frederick Dobbs, a 28-year-old applied sciences instructor who had gained experience as the head of the lubricating department of the Vacuum Oil Company; George Morris, a forging instructor who had tempered his talents through years of work at the Bath Iron Works and the Boston Navy Yard; and Ernest Amy, head of the Carpentry and Building Department, who came from Straight University in New Orleans, where he had been superintendent of the Industrial Department.

An eager flock of 244 students wait for the doors to open on the first day of classes, September 25, 1911. Despite appearances, hats were not specifically mandated.

"This first group of professors," wrote C.D. Brown, MC&TD '13, "was a group of young, energetic men. They even spent the night before opening day placing electric lights in the fixtures, and otherwise preparing for the first day's classes."

On that opening day—September 25, 1911—244 students walked through the doors of Wentworth Institute. Throughout the brand-new West Building and Power Plant, boilers were fired up, lathes were turned, and patterns were molded for the first of countless times. Eight-and-a-half years after he wrote the words in his final will and testament, Arioch Wentworth's dream to "furnish education in the mechanical arts" had finally become a reality.

HONESTY, ENERGY, ECONOMY, SYSTEM

Arthur Williston believed strongly in educating the whole person. The opportunities to do so, however, were limited at a specialized one- and two-year school such as Wentworth Institute. So, Williston seized upon Arioch Wentworth's family crest as a useful staging ground for rounding out students' moral and ethical education. He based the Institute's seal on the Wentworth family's heraldic shield, framed by four banners, each bearing a fundamental virtue: honesty, energy, economy, and system. Contemporaries of Arioch Wentworth told Williston that the founder had placed great stock in these virtues during his lifetime.

The first of several iterations the Wentworth seal would undergo in the 20th century. Its main ingredients, however, have remained constant. Central among these is the scroll of four virtues held dear by Arioch Wentworth: Honesty, Energy, Economy, and System.

Principal Williston wrote in 1920:

"This seal presents to us, like the knights of old, a challenge to battle royal for the development of these qualities of personality, which are essential in America in the year 1920 as truly as at any previous time in any foreign land. For Wentworth men, the period for self-development is unusually brief, but the goal is high. The practical and concrete nature of all our courses of instruction must not and does not blind us to the fact that our aim is preparation for life—the real life of our generation, in which manhood and capacity for service are predominant. These are the four-square qualities of manhood for which the seal of Wentworth Institute would inspire us all to strive:

- *Honesty*, in thought, in word, and in deed, that sees with precision things as they are, that speaks fearlessly without selfishness or malice, and that acts always with confident straightforwardness;
- *Energy*, of mind and body, that comes with the full development of all our powers and the ability to concentrate them all at will;
- *Economy*, steadfast and constant, that is the natural product of the exercise of sound judgment, self-restraint, and self-denial, and;
- *System*, the cultivated habit of orderly and well-considered procedure in thought and in conduct."

Even today in the 21st century, the seal continues to be the strongest symbol of the moral and ethical underpinnings of Wentworth's educational mission. Its virtues provide the foundation for the Wentworth Creed that guides current students.

BUILDING THE CAMPUS

The construction of campus buildings proceeded at a steady and determined pace under Williston's watchful eye. The West Building's foundation had just been dug when Williston arrived in the fall of 1910. Right away, he impressed upon the architects his desire for how this building should relate to the Main Building, which would be completed in 1914, and the East Building (a mirror image of the West Building), which would go up in 1916.

The architects laid out these three buildings to fulfill Williston's wishes, which were strikingly similar to those of a chain gang boss. The layout, for instance, compelled students to enter and exit solely through the central door of the Main Building, the first floor of which housed administrative offices. Williston wrote, "It is believed that this central control of the student body is similar in a way to the control obtained in a large manufacturing plant. Students cannot enter or leave the buildings without passing the general offices. They are obliged to pass the general bulletin boards at least twice daily. Habitual tardiness is easily observed and corrected."

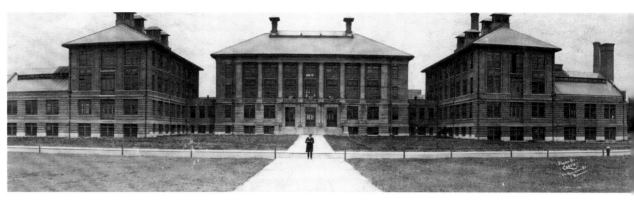

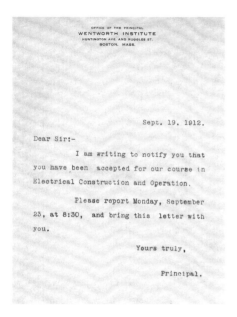

OFFICE OF THE PRINCIPAL
WENTWORTH INSTITUTE
HUNTINGTON AVE. AND RUGGLES ST.
BOSTON, MASS.

Sept. 19, 1912.

Dear Sir:-

I am writing to notify you that you have been accepted for our course in Electrical Construction and Operation.

Please report Monday, September 23, at 8:30, and bring this letter with you.

Yours truly,

Principal.

Above: A September 19, 1912, acceptance letter for a student in the electrical construction and operation program. Principal Williston's terseness underscores the no-frills personality that defined Wentworth Institute from day one.

Top: The two premier commissions from Peabody & Stearns' body of work between 1911 and 1916. Left, the Custom House tower; right, Wentworth Institute's main complex, circa 1916.

This three-building complex blended academic Classical Revival elements with tapestry brick surface treatments—a stylistic mix, according to the Boston Landmarks Commission, used frequently for industrial and institutional construction between 1910 and 1930. The architects, Peabody & Stearns, also nodded toward the massive institutional neighbor across the street—the Museum of Fine Arts, which had been built in 1908. To this day, Wentworth's main complex, with its U-shaped layout and monumental columns, looks like the MFA's brawny younger brother.

Peabody & Stearns ranked among the finest architects in Boston during the early decades of the 20th century. At the same time these architects were working on Wentworth's Main Building in 1914, they were also busy designing a building that remains one of Boston's most treasured landmarks: the Custom House tower.

By 1916, six years after the first shovel turned over earth on the campus, Wentworth Institute consisted of four imposing buildings that contained 18 laboratories, a dozen classrooms and drawing rooms, a foundry, library, and assembly hall, and the means to supply heat and power to all the above.

A SCHOOL THAT WORKS

The directors of Wentworth Institute could not have asked for a better first decade. Enrollments in daytime courses climbed steadily the first several years— from 244 the opening year to 652 ten years later. The numbers soared to greater heights in the evening school. By the early '20s, more than 1,000 men each year studied at Wentworth during nighttime hours.

The most pleasant surprise for the directors was the unexpected popularity of two-year courses. Before the Institute opened, the directors had assumed that most students would wish to dedicate no more than one year to academic pursuits. It turned out otherwise. The quality of the Institute had a lot to do with it. True, many students had intended to complete just a one-year course, after which they'd commence with the salary-earning portion of their lives. But having enjoyed their experience so much during the first year, hundreds of young men decided to re-up for a second year at Wentworth, and transferred to a two-year offering.

The directors and Williston deserve credit for shaping their curriculum wisely. Each program they settled on gained a devoted following. Three majors in particular—architectural construction, electrical construction and operation, and machine construction and tool design—garnered so many applications each year that the Institute was forced to cap enrollments.

One thing was for sure—students weren't enrolling because Wentworth Institute was such a lark. Quite the opposite, in fact. One student who had enrolled after a 15-year career as a machinist noted that the Wentworth instructors worked him harder than any employer ever had.

Students enrolled because the benefits so quickly became clear. A Wentworth education worked. Right away, the school gained a first-rate reputation in the industrial Northeast. (Charles Vaughn, a 1912 electric wiring graduate, told this story about the hunt for his first job: "I went into an electrical contractor's place one morning and they asked me what I had been doing. I told them that I had been attending an electrical school. They said that they had no confidence in the men that were being turned out by electrical schools. They asked me what school I had attended. I said, 'Wentworth Institute.' They said, 'That's different, come around tomorrow.'") By 1914, in fact, Principal Williston had to scramble to create a new staff position: placement director. George Pierce, EC&O '13, took the job and, from day one, local firms and factories queued up outside his door to bid on the services of Wentworth graduates. Pierce once joked that he knew the hiring manager at the New England Telephone & Telegraph Company better than he knew his own wife.

Below left: A go-go advertisement that ran in Boston newspapers in 1912. "You like tools and machinery—that's why this ad attracted your attention. Now then—let's get results. Mechanical work is mighty interesting. And it pays good money!" The real eye-catcher, though, was the $6-per-term tuition fee.

Below right: Members of the 1915 pattern making class show off their wares on the front steps of the Main Building. Note how young some of the students look.

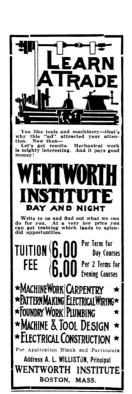

Antithesis of the Soup Line

"Every night at Avery Street, 400 or 500 men, out of employment and unable to find it, form a line to wait their turn for a bowl of hot soup given by public-spirited philanthropy. If you were to visit their line any night you would find in it many self-respecting men willing and anxious to work, who have been driven to the extremity of accepting public charity. The picture of them is as depressing and harrowing as any sight to be found in our city.

"Wentworth Institute, I say, stands for the antithesis of this Avery Street soup line. The soup line exists because these men have not the skill to do the kind of work that the world needs, and at present there is no demand for their services."

—Arthur L. Williston
March 19, 1914

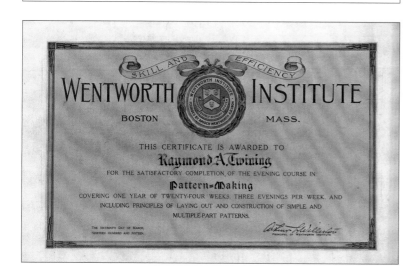

Above: A certificate earned by Raymond A. Twining, a 1916 graduate of the evening pattern making program.

Above right: Twining is the student at left, representing his alma mater at a 1916 industrial exhibition in Mechanics' Hall in Boston.

Right: A potpourri of patterns, 1915.

How the First Class Fared

On March 1, 1913, 29 members of the Class of 1912 gathered for the first-ever alumni banquet. These were the true trailblazers—graduates of the opening run of the Institute's one-year courses. Each man recounted his experience since leaving Wentworth Institute the year before.

Carpentry & Building

Albert N. Clark: Went to work with my father. Found it easy to get along with him; but to show him the new way of doing things you have got to prove it before you can do it. I can always convince him in the long run. If the Institute taught more carpentry and less cabinet making, it would help out a lot.

Elmer A. Crowell: Got so much out of last year that I returned to take another year.

Charles E. Hennessey: Went to work as a substitute letter carrier during the summer and returned to Wentworth in the fall to take up plumbing.

R.E. Morrison: I worked at carpentry during the summer, but then returned to the school last fall for another year. I am now at work on a $2,000 contract for alterations in a store. One of the graduates of the electric wiring course worked on the store's wiring.

Electric Wiring

John Cullen: I went around to one place after another, and finally went to work for the New England Telephone & Telegraph Company, where I am now.

W.H. Edgar: I got employment with the Telephone Company. They wanted to know just what sort of men the new school was turning out. Everyone there was interested in the school and seemed to know all about it. They wanted to know some of the things I had learned, such as Ohm's Law. When I was able to tell them some of the things and demonstrate that I know them, they had more respect for the school than ever. The school is making a good impression, I find.

Errol C. Hayes: When I went looking for a job, the contractors all wanted to know what I had been doing. I told them I had been attending Wentworth Institute. Things didn't pan out very good. At last I got a chance with an electrical clock company, but the firm was bought out by the trust and I was thrown out of work. I'm now working for an electrical contractor in Melrose. Most of the work is old house work and I don't have much experience with that kind of work. On new house work, I'm all right.

L.H. Nation: I'm with the Edison Company. I've found that the school has done me a great deal of good.

Robert A. Tibbetts: Mr. Mayo secured me a place with an electrical firm. They seemed to think a great deal of Wentworth Institute. They intend to give my job to some other Wentworth graduate this year, and advance me to something better.

Charles H. Vaughn: I went into an electrical contractor's place one morning and they asked me what I had been doing. I told them that I had been attending an electrical school. They said that they had no confidence in the men that were being turned out by electrical schools. They asked me what school I had attended. I said, "Wentworth Institute." They said, "That's different, come around tomorrow." But that afternoon, I secured a job as assistant electrician at Whalen Park, a summer theater in the central part of the state. The next morning the electrical concern telephoned me to come to work, but I told them I already had a job.

Foundry Practice

Ralph E. Briggs: I persuaded Mr. Johnson that I'd be better off if I came back for another year. Couldn't bear to leave this place. I've returned for the advanced course and am doing some very interesting work.

Benjamin C. Newhall: I went to work in a foundry during the summer and made good pay. I liked the place and am going back there next June, after I've finished a year of advanced work at the Institute.

H.M. Swasey: I went to work in Lawrence at a foundry, the owner of which was a special day and evening student at the Institute last year. I gave up my job in September and returned to school for an advanced course in foundry.

William Towle: I didn't like it when I was thrown into the foundry course, but found it better than I thought it would be. I've returned to the Institute to take machine construction.

J.R. White: Worked only a short time, but what I learned at Wentworth Institute meant a great deal to me and helped me get along. In the fall I went to the New Bedford Textile School.

The first class of Wentworth graduates, May 1912. The students perched on the window ledges lend a sense of chaos seldom witnessed at the Institute.

Machine Work

A.V. Chase: I went to work in a foundry after I graduated and worked there until it burned down. Don't like foundry work, however, and am back to the school taking machine work.

Henry C. Lord: Took a vacation and returned to school.

Gustave F. Neuberger: After I graduated I stayed around the house a while until my father told me he thought it was time I was doing something. So I worked for six weeks fixing up around my father's place. Then I decided I would have to really go to work, so I got a job, but the hours were from 5:45 in the morning till 9:00 at night. I decided this was too strenuous and gave the job up. At last I received a telephone call from the office of the Institute to go to work in a drafting room, and it was just the kind of a job I wanted. I get a good variety of work, and the work is interesting. Most of the work is for the government and it goes to Washington to be checked up. I'm now taking the evening drawing course at the Institute.

Albert Schweig: When I went to Wentworth I did not know the difference between a drill press and a lathe. After I graduated I worked in a machine shop until October, at which time I asked for a raise and got it. A short time ago I asked for another raise. I got it today. School has been a great help to me.

Pattern Making

George F. Elliott: Too small to get a job, so took a vacation and returned to school for advanced course.

G.R. Howard: Broke up the car strike and returned to school for advanced course.

Lloyd A. Phelan: After graduating, I got a job in a drafting room, but after a while I found that I couldn't get what I wanted so I picked out a place where I thought I'd like to work and asked them for a job. I told them I came from Wentworth and they seemed to be interested. I went in there every Saturday for a month. The last time I called they told me they were just holding a directors' meeting to decide whether they would take me on.

Harry T. Schult: Went to work in a pattern shop on Atlantic Avenue, but work got dull so I returned to the Institute for advanced work.

Harold W. Souther: I found that I was too small to go to work, so I decided to take a long vacation and go back to school.

William C. Studdiford: I went to 15 places and was turned down in every place before I finally succeeded in securing a job as a pattern maker with the Draper Company in Hopedale. I have worked in four different places as a journeyman pattern maker. I am getting by all right.

The 1912 plumbing class.

Plumbing

W.L. McKenna: Started in with my father. I got a great deal of practical knowledge in the school and have had a chance to apply it since. Did not get as much practical work with my father as I wanted, as I was taken in from the outside work and sent to estimating. I have signed up two schools and a theater in Dorchester. Now I have to lay out all work on these buildings. Experience that I got at Wentworth Institute is proving very valuable. Comparison with ordinary laborers shows that if they'd had the same opportunities as me, they would be very much more advanced than they are now. Many plumbers have come to me for advice on certain parts of the work and I've shown them their mistakes. The only proper advice that I could give them was, "Go to Wentworth and learn how to do things right."

Eddy Nichols: Went out as a helper but thought better of it and went into business for myself. Have not got stuck yet. Cannot tell when I will get stuck. Learned a good deal at Wentworth.

D.J. O'Connor: Went to work for my father, who is in the plumbing business. My course at Wentworth helped me a great deal in my work. Have had many arguments with my father as to the best methods of doing work. My father has to be shown, but I've satisfied him a great many times that the Wentworth Institute methods are the best.

William C. Ogden: I had worked as a helper for a couple of years before coming to the Institute. Shortly after graduating I received word from the office to go out to Jamaica Plain and look up a job there. I am still on the job. I think that my training at the Institute put me at least two years ahead. My greatest handicap is in laying out work. I am taking up drawing in the Evening School this year. I am very grateful for all that I received at the school.

5. Kenrick Baker, PM '13
The Alumnus

A direct descendant of famed Pilgrim John Alden, Kenrick Baker himself stands as the symbolic ancestor of generations of Wentworth alumni. A

member of the second class to graduate from Wentworth, Baker in 1920 became the first president of the Alumni Association and the first alumnus elected to the Institute's board of directors. His 55-year tenure on the board (1920–1975) remains the longest in Wentworth's history. Two principals and two presidents relied on Baker to represent the sensibilities of alumni as the board set the course for Wentworth during a span of six decades. "Ken lived and breathed Wentworth," said a colleague on the board. Even Baker's day job aligned closely with the Institute's mission. For 44 years he directed vocational education at Brockton High School, a job that allowed him to steer hundreds of young men toward furthering their education at Wentworth. In 1972, the Institute dedicated its brand-new dormitory on Huntington Avenue in Baker's name.

6. Albert L. Harlow, MW '14
The War Hero

Thousands of Wentworth alumni are veterans of war. Nearly 100 of them lost their lives in the course of serving their country. The first Went-

worth graduate to die on the battlefield was actually a Canadian. Albert Harlow of Nova Scotia earned a certificate in machine work from Wentworth Institute in 1914. He enlisted a year later and embarked for England on July 23, 1916. In March 1917, he was sent to France as part of England's "Fighting 25th" infantry battalion. He died on November 8, 1917, near Passchendaele, Belgium. A comrade's letter to Harlow's father told the horrible story: "Word came down from the line for six men from each section to go out and get some of our wounded men. Your son and I picked up a stretcher and started on our struggle. We found eight men in a hole of water, very badly wounded, who had been there two days with nothing to eat. Four of us picked up one

man and started for the dressing station. After an awful time, we got this man out and started back for another. By this time, it was daylight and the Huns saw us and opened heavy shells on us. So we all ran for shelter by an old pillbox, but could not get out of the fire. Two shells landed right on top of us. I knew nothing for a while. When I came to, there was no one standing but myself."

7. Wesley Packard, MC&TD '25
The Machinist

When one reflects on the machine shop at Wentworth, certain constants come to mind: castor oil to keep the parts cranking, belts to keep the gears churning, and Wes Packard to keep the whole operation humming. Raised on a dairy

farm in Newington, N.H., Packard traded udders for lathes in 1922 when he enrolled in the Institute's machine construction and tool design program. After graduating in 1925, he became an instructor in the machine shop. In 1955, he was promoted to head of the department, a job he kept until his retirement in 1967. The Institute never knew a more devoted teacher than Packard; Wes made a point to spend his summers working in industry so that he could better prepare his students upon returning to Wentworth in the fall.

8. George Pierce, EC&O '13
The Registrar

George Pierce oversaw the efficient day-to-day operation of academic affairs during the Institute's first half-century. After completing his

studies as a member of Wentworth's first electrical construction and operation class, he served 42 years as registrar for the day school. Here, his exacting precision and systematic record keeping sustained the Institute during the enrollment of tens of thousands of students. Each of these students knew that, practically speaking, all roads led through George Pierce. In the tightly regimented world of Wentworth, Pierce wielded awesome power as registrar. In students' eyes, he

represented the line between oppression and freedom. If a student wanted to leave campus during lunch hour, for instance, Mr. Pierce was the sole arbiter. Or, as one alumnus remembers, "if you wanted to escape early on Friday before the Christmas holiday, you practically had to sign your life away to Pierce."

9. Vojtech Preissig
The Printmaker

Head of Wentworth Institute's School of Printing and Graphic Arts from 1917 to 1924, Vojtech Preissig produced a body of work still held in

high regard by graphic designers today. A citizen of Czechoslovakia, Preissig was a gifted printmaker. He had an artist's temperament, which rarely squared well with the conservative leadership of Principal Arthur Williston. "I cannot be head of a department only to be the tool or fool of a principal," Preissig wrote angrily to a friend in 1921. Disgruntlement aside, his impressive talent remains evident to this day. Whereas Williston considered printmaking a trade, Preissig refused to regard it as anything but an art. Eighty years later, many of the works his Wentworth classes produced—departmental posters or the school's World War I Honor Roll—reinforce Preissig's point of view. After the department head left Wentworth Institute, he returned to his homeland, where he merged his knack for printmaking with a passionate patriotism. Tragically, his propaganda posters made him an early target for the Nazis. Vojtech Preissig died on November 6, 1944, in the Dachau concentration camp.

10. Vincent B. Robinson, MW '13, MC&TD '14
The Pioneer

Institute records tell us precious little about alumnus Vincent Robinson. But these facts we know: He, along with 23 classmates, earned a

machine work certificate in 1913 as part of the second class to graduate from Wentworth Institute. Upon leaving Wentworth, he secured a job as a machinist in Providence, R.I. Like countless thousands of other

Wentworth grads, he lived a good, solid life. He died in 1952. But it's one last fact about Vincent Robinson that makes him noteworthy: He was the first black student to graduate from Wentworth.

11. George Tapp, MW '13
The Welder

For graduates from Wentworth's first 45 years, one phrase rang loud in their collective memory:

"Heat it up, lads!" These words, bellowed at high volume, were the mantra of forging and welding instructor George Tapp. A 1913 graduate of the machine work program, Tapp brought an intense teaching style to the basement of the Shop Building. In the eyes of many students, his pithy instructions ("Spit on it before you pick it up," for instance) ascended to the level of life-altering philosophy. "His words stayed with me forever," said alumnus Ernest Curwen, MW '21, EC '23. "I don't know how much I learned about forging, but I sure did learn that to do a job right, you've got to HEAT-IT-UP, figuratively. Whenever one of my projects got bogged down, I'd think of Mr. Tapp and his famous words, then back to the drawing board I'd go for new and better ideas." As a young instructor, Tapp taught machine work to a group of World War I recruits who became the 101st Engineers. Tapp signed on with the Regiment when it left for France in September 1917. He served as a horseshoer and master engineer in Company B until the unit was discharged in April 1919. Back on campus, his influence lingers to this day in charming ways. Tapp's hands wrought the lighting fixtures in Watson Auditorium as well as the ornate iron grillwork that adorns the stairwells on either side of Wentworth Hall's main lobby.

12. Arthur L. Williston
The Builder

Arthur Lyman Williston came to Wentworth Institute in 1910 with the reputation of an "edu-

cational architect." He demonstrated these skills abundantly during his 12 years as the Institute's first principal. First of all, he supervised the construction of Wentworth's three core buildings—facilities that remain the nucleus of the campus 94 years later. Even more important, he collaborated with the Institute's directors to build a curriculum from the ground up. The directors had chosen Williston with this in mind: from 1898 to 1910, he had headed the School of Science and Technology at Pratt Institute in Brooklyn, New York. Williston was a stern, no-nonsense administrator. Student attendance was a particular obsession; he constantly hectored his instructors to take a harder line. The principal was hands-on as well. From the time students first enrolled in 1911, he insisted on personally interviewing every applicant for admission. This meant about 750 interviews each year. The establishment of wartime training at Wentworth from 1917 to 1918 put Williston's organizational abilities to perfect use. He took great pride in contributing the Institute's resources to the patriotic effort. In the years following the war, the principal's enthusiasm in overseeing the day-to-day affairs of the Institute flagged, and he delegated more and more responsibility to his assistant, Frederick Dobbs. Williston resigned in 1923 and spent the last three decades of his life as an educational consultant. He wrote at length about engineering education; in 1944, he authored a book, *Beyond the Horizon of Science*. In 1952, the American Society for Engineering Education chose Williston as the third recipient of its prestigious James H. McGraw Award. In addition, the ASEE named its annual award for writing excellence in his honor.

BLANCHE HALL, A TEACHER OF MANUAL TRAINING, IS WENTWORTH'S FORGOTTEN PIONEER. IN 1919, 53 YEARS BEFORE WOMEN WERE OFFICIALLY ADMITTED TO WENTWORTH, MISS HALL COMPLETED AN INFORMAL COURSE RUN BY THE SCHOOL OF PRINTING AND GRAPHIC ARTS.

Vojtech Preissig, center, led the School of Printing and Graphic Arts from 1917 to 1924. The print shop, with its sometimes noxious fumes (note the vent hood), operated on the top floor of the East Building (Dobbs Hall today).

Clockwise from right:
The 1916-17 basketball
team; 1917 baseball team;
and 1916 baseball team.

ONE YEAR AT WENTWORTH: DOES IT PAY?

"As the scholastic year draws to a close each spring at Wentworth Institute, several hundred young men receive the parting instructions and preparation for their chosen occupations; and of the many who completed their courses last June, Ralph Schaller has a right to be proud of his record both at the Institute and after graduation.

Schaller attended the Institute for the season of 1920-21 and proved to be an apt student, who by constant diligence absorbed much knowledge of the theory and practice of plumbing. When he went out as an alumnus in June 1921, he did so with the determination to succeed at his trade and to advance beyond it. With the energy and ambition characteristic of most Wentworth graduates, he allowed no time to elapse before going up for the state examination for journeyman plumber, and on June 9th he received his license. Five days later, less than a week after the closing of school, he went out on a job.

For the first five weeks, he worked for $41.90 per week and earned a total of $209.50. This brought him up to the 21st of July, when he went to Lowell where he worked for three months and earned $501.45 during that time. On the 21st of October, when his work on this job was completed, Schaller packed up his tools to seek another job. Nor did he have to wait long; for he found a job on the same day and started in to work again with as much perseverance as ever, sticking to the job till it was finished on the 2nd of December. On being paid off, he found that his earnings were $144.00.

During the first six months after his graduation, Schaller earned a total of $854.48. Accordingly, on the $45 that he invested in tuition for a one-year course at the Institute, he is receiving interest at the rate of 950 percent per annum. For these six months, Schaller's living expenses averaged $8.50 per week, so that the net profit for his labor for the half-year after leaving the Institute was $641.98.

Such perfect service, however, has not only a monetary reward, but it brings the doer a satisfaction of mind and establishes a reputation for industry well worth having."

—Tekton, Spring 1922

Below: A 1917 plumbing class. "The health of the community is dependent on sanitary plumbing," read the 1917-18 catalog, "and the modern plumber should know the principles of hydraulics and sanitation."

Bottom: Students operate a printing press in the East Building, 1920.

TECHNICAL INSTITUTES: A BRIEF HISTORY

Arthur L. Williston invented the term, "technical institute," at a conference held in Rochester, N.Y., in 1922. So, it's no surprise that he later became the most knowledgeable historian of such organizations. In 1948, he wrote the defining essay, "The Technical Institute in America."

According to Williston, the concept of technical institutes dated back to the second half of the 19th century. As industrialism took hold in America, so too did the "efforts to produce industrial intelligence and ideals of excellence in production among a selected group of young men."

As a boy growing up in Cambridge, Massachusetts, Williston had been greatly influenced by an early example of just such an initiative. In the late 1870s, his parents had enrolled him in a Saturday-morning woodworking program recently begun in the basement of a police station. A group of individuals had provided the equipment and hired an instructor. This program developed into the Rindge Manual Training School, and later, the Rindge Technical High School.

A more influential development along these lines, wrote Williston, was the introduction in 1875 "of the shop practice into schools of engineering, stimulated by the display of the Russian system at the Philadelphia Exposition."

Undertakings such as these shared characteristics that would soon become paramount features of the educational philosophy of technical institutes:

- The instruction was largely individual.
- It was given to persons who appeared to have probable capacity for industrial leadership or efficiency.
- The aim was toward creative industrial intelligence and knowledge of the current processes of industrial production in special fields.

In the late part of the 19th century and early years of the 20th, many institutions of higher education were founded in a manner loyal to the "technical institute" brand of instruction, but over time departed from that approach: Drexel Institute

Below: For 25 years, the School of Printing and Graphic Arts produced all of Wentworth Institute's printed materials, including this self-promotional piece.

Below right: A 1917 typography class. The pedestal desks were not standard issue at the Institute; Vojtech Preissig had requested them specially for the School of Printing and Graphic Arts.

in Philadelphia, Cooper Union in New York City, and the Armour and Lewis Institutes of Chicago were three prominent examples. Williston bemoaned this tendency for institutions to "slip and retrograde from the high level of creative leadership to the level of the usual and the commonplace, where the shop practice loses all creative and inspirational value and becomes routine handicraft instruction devoid of insight into the marvels of American production."

In contrast, other technical institutes stayed true to their founding philosophy. The four best examples, according to Williston, were Rochester Institute of Technology, Franklin Technical Institute in Boston, Pratt Institute's School of Science and Technology, and Wentworth Institute.

Why were these schools the cream of the crop? Because, wrote Williston, they remained loyal adherents to each of these 14 distinctive traits of a technical institute:

- The instruction centers upon the individual student.
- The latent or potential talents and aptitudes of each student are sought and revealed.
- Probable ultimate fitness for a calling or a specific type of job is made the chief criterion for admission to each course of instruction.
- The instruction capitalizes each young man's ambition for particular achievement or for the attainment of some special goal.
- Elements of the real work of the world are used as instruments of training.
- Progress of pupils is appraised by visible and definite achievements.
- The requirements are carefully adjusted to the abilities and capacities of each pupil.
- Steps in the instruction or between assigned tasks are short enough to be readily mastered and to prevent confusion in thought.
- Thus, speed and precision are encouraged.
- New experiences are related to old in such a manner that the pupil draws valid conclusions and himself arrives at new principles.
- Memory disciplines are subordinated to creative thinking and constructive action.
- Throughout, a professional attitude is sought, sometimes expressed by the slogan, "A passion for superlative excellence and the consecration of one's trained talents in the service of mankind."
- Conditions are created that foster those qualities of personality that result in leadership.
- Habits are encouraged in both conduct and thinking that are helpful in meeting the requirements of future occupations.

Williston wrapped up his 1948 essay by speaking not about history or theory, but about an alarming crisis: "In the place of one or two score of technical institutes in the United States, there should be at least one thousand scattered throughout the country furnishing training for fully half of the youth in our population. This obviously is the *missing link* in our educational system."

WENTWORTH IN THE NATION'S SERVICE: World War I

In the spring of 1917, Wentworth Institute was still finding its way. The fledgling school had just concluded its sixth year of instruction in the mechanical arts, in deference to Arioch Wentworth's wishes as founder. In a flash, however, it began moonlighting as an instructor in military arts, in deference to President Woodrow Wilson's wishes as commander in chief.

The role the Institute played during World War I marked perhaps the finest hour of its first 100 years. Over the course of 18 months, Wentworth trained 4,077 men for war service, molded an entire corps of military engineers, and transformed its college grounds into a secure training encampment. In the process, the Institute came of age virtually overnight as an educational institution.

On April 6, 1917, Congress voted for the United States to join the fighting in The Great War. Four weeks later, on May 3, Wentworth Institute received a visit from Colonel F.L. Joy of the First Corps of Cadets. This Massachusetts infantry battalion, Joy explained to Principal Arthur Williston, had an honorable 176-year history but an unpromising future. American forces had already started to ship over to France, but the Cadets didn't seem to figure into the government's master plan. So, Joy plotted a makeover that would make his men indispensable to the War Department. Recognizing a void within the National Guard of New England, the Cadets wanted to qualify as an engineering regiment, and then seek acceptance in the U.S. Army.

Camp Wentworth, photographed hours after 101st Engineers recruits finished pitching 100 tents on the Institute's triangular lot (home today to Sweeney Field).

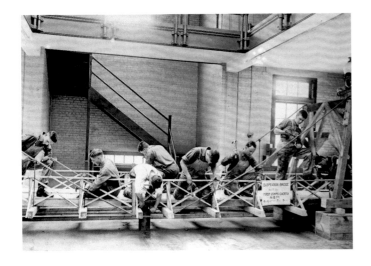

Military engineering skills in the embryonic stage.

Above: Recruits build a 50-foot-long suspension bridge.

Above right: Barrack construction on Parker Street (Boston Trade High School is visible at rear).

Below: A machine gun emplacement where Beatty Hall stands today. It took four men 22 hours to build it.

An excellent idea, save for a few problems. At the time, the Cadets consisted of about 300 civilian volunteers, very few of whom possessed any specific engineering or technical expertise. Moreover, these men had access to neither the equipment nor the instructors by which to learn the necessary skills.

Colonel Joy's original intent in visiting Wentworth was simply to deliver a recruiting pitch to the Institute's students, any of whom would have been a welcome addition to a shorthanded corps of military engineers. But, a few minutes into their initial meeting in Williston's office, the colonel and the principal devised a dramatically different plan.

Wentworth Institute agreed to place its facilities, equipment, and instructors at the disposal of the First Corps of Cadets. Incredibly, the work began just 72 hours later. On May 7, 1917, 300 cadets marched from the Armory on Columbus Avenue to Wentworth Institute for the beginning of evening courses. The instruction needed to take place in the evening because these men had not yet been mustered into service and, therefore, were still working at their normal daytime jobs.

Each soldier chose one of eight hastily arranged courses in which he wished to train. They were:

- Wooden structures, bridges, and timbering;
- Concrete construction, with special reference to trench protection, dugouts, and bomb-proof foundations;
- Structural drafting;
- Mechanical drafting, applied to military equipment;

A handful of recruits who focused on "motor truck repair." The truck shown here was built up and torn apart several times as part of the training at Wentworth Institute.

- Generation and distribution of electricity for field purposes;
- Gas engines and generation of power;
- Forging and acetylene welding; and
- Machine work for emergency repairs.

Wentworth instructors led each of the courses. The timing was right. Normally, when the school year ended, these men spent the summer working part time in whatever industry pertained to their teaching. With war declared, however, Principal Williston needed to twist no arms to persuade his faculty to dedicate the appropriate time to summer teaching.

The curriculum featured no frills and harbored no pretensions. "The time is too short to give any elaborate theoretical training," noted Williston. "The instruction must be given through very brief and intensive courses and given in a very practical way." The end result, hoped the principal, would be a highly functional group of "embryo-engineers."

An acetylene welder was "a tool of the utmost importance for repair in the field," according to Regiment commanders.

From the moment training began in early May, the Corps' recruiting efforts caught fire. During the program's first couple of weeks, 40 to 50 new men arrived each night at Wentworth to begin instruction. By June, the Corps had swelled to 800 men. For eight-and-a-half weeks, this first wave of soldiers spent four hours a night molding themselves into battle-ready engineers.

On July 5, after completing 36 sessions, the company boarded a train for Camp Devens in Ayer, Mass., where they spent two months supplementing their newfound engineering skills with more intense military training.

At this time, the U.S. government sent an inspector to Wentworth to assess the merits of its training, and was pleased with the ensuing report. As a result, the War Department asked the Institute to expand its offerings. On July 25, President Wilson mustered the National Guard of Massachusetts into full-time service. This freed up the recruits' daytime hours for training purposes,

Above: The Regiment's daily "sick report" noted 16 incidents of "blistered hands" on the day after the first lesson in trench design and construction.

Right: "Many hands make light work" as footings are dug for the temporary barracks on Parker Street.

Above: The September 23, 1917, "graduation" of 834 non-commissioned officers and enlisted men of the 101ˢᵗ Regiment of Engineers.

Top: U.S. Army Training Detachment, November 13, 1918, two days after the Armistice was signed.

and Wentworth jumped without hesitation into its second round of training.

Seven hundred new recruits to the engineering regiment arrived in late July. They were organized into 14 groups of 50 men, each focusing on one aspect of field or shop work. Field courses included trench design and construction, field telephony, and highway building and railroad construction. Shop courses included blacksmithing, military mapping and sketching, and internal combustion engine repair.

After two weeks, the logistics of shuttling in 700 men each day grew too cumbersome. On August 5, Wentworth received notice that camp needed to be set up on the Institute's grounds. Immediately, the recruits pitched 100 tents on either side of Ruggles Street. (Folks called it "Camp Wentworth.") Mess tents were placed along Parker Street. Armed guards patrolled the Institute's grounds 24 hours a day, and special passes were required to enter or exit the campus. This was manageable during the summer but when September arrived, Williston requested permission to relax the access rules a bit so as not to intimidate Wentworth's tuition-paying students during the hectic registration week for the 1917-18 school year.

The training spanned an intense eight-and-a-half weeks. Every classroom and laboratory in the Institute's four buildings was filled with young men learning some component of military engineering. In the Power Plant, men tinkered with gasoline engines; in the construction laboratory, recruits mixed the concrete and tested the lumber that would shore up trenches and dugouts; and in the foundry, men forged the eye-bolts, rings, and chains that riggers would use in the field. Outside, men dug trenches where Beatty Hall stands today; tamped ties and drove spikes on Huntington Avenue for the Boston Elevated Railway Company; and drew freehand topographical maps during a roundtrip ride to Billerica, Mass., aboard a motorcycle sidecar.

One newspaper account related how "nurses and old gentlemen who liked to take early morning constitutionals through the shady walks of the Fenway were often severely startled to run across khaki-clad figures lying face down or perched in trees, even wading the river and bounding rabbit-like across the narrow paths of the park, notebook and pencil in hand, and all the time with their eyes glued on some distant object. For a while, the Fenway began to get the name of being a dangerous place. But now it is well known that these were merely agile young military engineers out on their first sketching expedition."

On September 23, 1917, the men were awarded certificates indicating their area of newly gained expertise. The next day, the entire Corps, which had reached the critical mass of 1,700 members, boarded a train to New York City. On September 26, the 101st Regiment of Engineers, as they now were called, embarked for France on the Cunard Steamship *Andania*.

Left: The certificate of 101st recruit, O.C. Turkington.

Below: Three soldiers mix concrete that will become the foundation of a portable power plant.

Below right: Tool repair.

France
January 1, 1918

My Dear Dobbs,

Gee but I was glad to get a letter from you and learn that you were interested enough in me to write. Glad, I should say so, and then some.

Also to know that things in general were on the jump at Wentworth, and the general Morris himself in command of the forge shop, with deputy Haskell. We're sure on the jump here in the construction end of things, and what; but I have a great old forge shop where four of us toil daily and I sleep nights. It's an antique French kitchen, open fireplace as they all are here, in fact. A great old place.

I'm as happy as can be—plenty of work, lots to eat, and well dressed, so what the hell do we care?

It's some wonderful experience; man, I would not trade it for a fortune. Rough and tough at times but then that's the joy of living.

Water systems, hospital work, in fact, everything, must be done to clear out this old French village and make it into a base by spring. And then what? Well, I hope someone will get hell as someone must pay for my being here, that's for sure.

Companies B & C are here, the others somewhere else. Captain Osborne is great on the job, does his work fine. Wentworth is hinted at many times in all connections.

The weather is real old Boston weather. Yes, and I built a double runner sled and the hills in this section are wonderful.

Visited some great old French towns and things are fairly backward and old-fashioned, but built to stand for years, as they sure have.

Missed the old New Year's Eve celebrations and the wild nights; but then someday, boy, I'll come back stronger than ever.

To all at the school, best wishes for the year ahead, and best to Mr. Williston. Would like to hear from you.

Yours,

Geo. Tapp

P.S. Any spare magazines around you could send?

[George Tapp graduated from the machine work program in 1913 and worked for many years at Wentworth Institute as a forging and welding instructor.]

Somewhere in France
December 10, 1917

Dear Mr. Dobbs,

A lull in the general rush of things, occasioned by a short stay in a hospital, gives me a chance to catch up with my correspondence. I have had it in mind many times to write to you but the opportunity never seemed to present itself.

Of course, I am not allowed to say just where we are or what we are doing, but I think the censor will pass the statement that two of us from each company are attending a certain school of instruction at the present time.

There is much to learn and the work is most interesting. What we learned at Wentworth is standing us in good stead but we also see that we might have made much more of the opportunities given us at your institution. As time goes on we can better appreciate the splendid thing that Wentworth Institute did for the Corps. Let us hope that some day we may be able to repay the debt in a fitting manner.

The excitement and confusion attending our departure prevented me from expressing my personal thanks to you and to your assistants for the obvious interest you so kindly showed in my own case. I am deeply grateful. Please tell Mr. Banks that the little French dictionary is my constant companion. Judging from the queer expressions on the faces of some of the people I try to talk with, I should say that my French must be a terrible thing to hear. But I am not discouraged.

I shall look forward to seeing you all on our return. Please give my best regards to all I know and, believe me, very sincerely yours.

John W. Condit

[John Condit was a member of the 101st Regiment of Engineers. Frederick Dobbs—see Chapter 4—was a Wentworth instructor.]

Above: Trucks haul the lumber for the barrack construction on the Wentworth campus.

Right: Cadets wire a telephone connection in a machine gunner's dugout.

Below: For 18 months, trucks had the run of the Wentworth quadrangle.

Wentworth Meets M.A.S.H.

101st Engineers Regiment Training
August 7, 1917

"Sick Report"

cuts: 7
blisters: 9
constipation: 3
strained arch: 1
burn: 1
faint: 1
ingrown toenail: 1
nose bleed: 1
dirt in eye: 3
acute indigestion: 1
sore throat: 2

"All treated and returned to duty."

Before departing, Major General Clarence R. Edwards expressed the Army's gratitude for Wentworth's assistance: "It gives me pleasure to acknowledge, with much appreciation, the patriotic and public spirit of the Institute in making the 101st Engineers into a practical engineering component of the 26th Division, United States Army. I believe these troops start with the making of as good an engineer regiment as will exist in the Army, and we owe much of it to you."

General Edwards' prediction of the troops' merits proved true. The 101st Engineers spent a year and a half in France and Belgium, in the heart of some of the fiercest fighting of the First World War. In 1919, the general wrote in praise, "I do not recall a single incident where the Regiment did not do better under emergency than I had reason to believe it could do. The Regiment had to organize, consolidate, change, and modify any number of sectors, always under shell fire and always subject to a breakthrough. It always did the job successfully, and like the veterans they proved themselves to be."

While the training of the 101st Engineers was Wentworth Institute's greatest contribution to the war effort, it was not, however, the last. In 1918, the school contracted with the federal government to offer a variety of similar

Below: A 1918 advertisement for a 12-week military training course.

Below right: National Army Training Detachment, 1918.

Above: Members of the 101st Engineers Regiment learn to rig a derrick, a necessity for moving heavy cargo on their mission overseas.

Top: Naval Training Detachment, 1918.

programs. For example, 160 members of the U.S. Navy took steam engineering classes at Wentworth. And the Army sent seven waves of recruits, ultimately totaling 1,610 men, to the Institute to learn specific trade and technical skills in a series of eight-week programs modeled after the 101st Engineers training. To house these Army recruits, the Institute converted its foundry wing and the third floor of the brand-new East Building (Dobbs Hall today) into barracks.

Principal Arthur Williston was the driving force behind Wentworth's extraordinary involvement with wartime instruction. In April 1918, U.S. Secretary of War Newton D. Baker appointed him as the educational director of training of drafted men in "industrial and mechanical lines." Williston's enthusiasm for the task was remarkable. A number of times he sent letters to the War Department that proposed expanding Wentworth Institute's involvement. Most of the time, Secretary Baker politely declined.

Even after the Armistice was signed on November 11, 1918, Williston and Wentworth Institute forged ahead with a progressive war-related initiative. In 1919, Wentworth ran free four-month courses to reintegrate veterans into productive civilian lives. "If it was worthwhile to train men to become specialists in destructive work," said Williston, "then it is far more worthwhile to train them for constructive work."

These veterans slept in the barracks still in place from the Institute's 1918 training programs. The principal directed the men toward fields where demand was outpacing supply, such as printing, pattern making, and plumbing. Dozens of the participants were physically disabled. But, as a newspaper article wrote, somewhat breezily, "the loss of a leg doesn't hamper a man much at a drafting board."

Paul Swanson, APM '20, greatly appreciated the program: "Just out of the Navy and not knowing what I wanted to do, I took advantage of the Institute's most generous offer and attended pattern making classes by day while availing myself of all the USO had to offer by night (dances, theater, etc.). I enrolled in the day school the next year and graduated with the advanced pattern making class in 1920. Department Head John Mickelson demanded near perfection in our shopwork and learning that alone has been a great help to me all my life."

Just a small number of the
4,077 World War I recruits
who trained at Wentworth
Institute.

WENTWORTH ALUMNI WHO DIED SERVING IN WORLD WAR I

"In memory of the Wentworth boys who gave their lives in the World War. That freedom and justice might prevail."

Edward J. Aldrich, EC '17

George C. Androvette, FP&O '18

James D. Arthur, MW '18

John J. Curley, PL '12

Ernest J. Ferranti, PL '18

Clifford B. Fletcher, PM '13, APM '14

Alfred F. Fowler, EW '16

Rollin W. Frey, FM&O '17

Charles G. Fyfe, TP '15

Harold W. Gallison, FM&O '18

Percy E. Glenn, PRTG '17

William O. Gordon, PL '18

Albert L. Harlow, MW '14

Henry L. Lamb, MC&TD '15

Stanley H. Luke, C&B '12

Malcolm B. Marsh, MW '18

Raybern B. Melendy, PM '14, APM '15

Alphonsus J. McGrath, EW '16

Andrew P. McLaughlin, EW '16

George R. McLeod, AC '16

Edward D. Newell, FP '12

Clyde N. Palmer, PM '17

Arthur E. Shiels, EW '12

Carlton J. Smith, EW '12

Edmund G. Tart, EC '14

William Towle, FP '12, MC&TD '14

Chester W. Ward, EC '20

Louis A. Young, MW '16

Above: William O. Gordon, PL '18.

Below: A simple white cross marks the site where Private George R. McLeod, AC '16, was buried in Guillemont, France.

Without question, patriotism fueled the veteran retraining initiative. An equally strong motivation, however, was the Institute's desire to honor the legacy of its alumni who served in the war.

Twenty-eight Wentworth graduates lost their lives in World War I. [*See list at left.*] In all, more than 800 alumni fought overseas. Their service record was admirable. Harold Kullberg, PM '15, MC&TD '17, was an apt representative. After the U.S. Air Service rejected him because he was so thin, Kullberg traveled to Canada and joined the Royal Flying Corps on April 21, 1917. Following a year of training at flying schools, he joined Squadron 1 in France. In three months time, he flew 280 hours over enemy lines and took part in more than 50 air battles. He brought down 14 German airplanes as well as two balloons. Promoted to deputy patrol leader in August, Kullberg was shot down a few days later behind enemy lines. With four bullet wounds in his leg, he managed to get his bearings on the ground, then reboarded his failing aircraft and flew back falteringly to American lines. After recuperating for six months in a Blighty hospital, he was discharged on July 31, 1919. Later, Kullberg was decorated with the Distinguished Flying Cross by the Prince of Wales in recognition of one engagement in which he encountered 10 German planes, brought down two, and put the other eight to flight.

As troops returned home in 1919 and the country returned to normal, Wentworth had found its stride as an educational institution. World War I had changed Wentworth Institute for the better. For one, it instilled a sense of purpose that the young school needed. By necessity, the Institute had spent the first few years of its existence arguing its worth to the region and the country. Its contributions during the war years, however, settled the matter once and for all. Moreover, the accelerated manner in which it was forced to train soldiers—emphasizing hands-on, practical applications—served to reinforce a teaching philosophy that continues to define the Institute to this day.

1924

1952

THE DOBBS ERA, 1924-1952

Top left: Wentworth's second principal, Frederick E. Dobbs.

Left: As a typical school day draws to a close in 1937, Wentworth students trek toward Huntington Avenue while cars motor by on Ruggles Street.

Below: Well-dressed students mill about on the steps in front of the Main Building, 1941.

At the close of the 1922-23 school year, Arthur Williston resigned as the principal of Wentworth Institute. Since the war, Williston's attention to the Institute had waned. He had, in fact, delegated many of the day-to-day duties to his assistant, Frederick Dobbs. That made Dobbs a natural choice for the directors when Williston departed. They appointed him principal in 1924.

The Dobbs era at Wentworth Institute reflected the qualities of the principal himself. Frederick Dobbs was an unassuming leader; solid and reliable, earnest and hard working. He certainly looked the part of principal. In the yearly faculty photograph, he stands out clearly. Tall and stately, sitting bolt upright; there's no mistaking who's the chief. His was a steady-hand principalship. The Institute made no earth-shattering changes during his 28–year tenure. But it did strengthen its position as one of the finest technical institutes in the country.

The Institute's first 100 years can be broken down to three general stages of development: trade school, two-year school, four-year school. The Dobbs era bore witness to the full maturation of stage one.

Dobbs' ego was virtually non-existent. Up to the very end of his time at Wentworth, he insisted on the title of principal, even though the more powerful title of president could have been his for the asking. He believed, however, that "president" would have been as much an overreach for him as was the idea of Wentworth becoming a degree-granting institution.

AN OLD-FASHIONED THINKER

Frederick Dobbs at his desk. George Washington's portrait hung on his wall, a fitting choice for a principal who proved he could stretch a dollar bill as far as anyone.

A visionary Dobbs was not. He was an able administrator but not a man of big ideas or grand strivings. In this regard he stood in contrast to the man who succeeded him in 1953, H. Russell Beatty. Dobbs mistrusted Beatty's ambitions. For example, he disapproved of Beatty's desire to be a president rather than a principal—in his mind, it signaled a hunger for power that he found distasteful. Moreover, it signaled that this new leader intended to recast the Institute a level higher than where Dobbs felt it should be.

For nearly 50 years, the Institute had gotten better and better at fulfilling the noble mission expressed by founder Arioch Wentworth. Why change now? thought Dobbs. Beatty's plans for the Institute, he believed, were ambitious but not necessarily wise.

Indeed, as President Beatty went on to reconfigure Wentworth Institute during the 1950s, Dobbs stayed true to his beliefs during his stint as an educational consultant for the Ford Foundation. He spent several years in Pakistan and India, transplanting the same style of technical institute he had overseen for 28 years at Wentworth.

At the Ford Foundation, Dobbs preached the merits of this "old-school" approach to technical education. He had good reason to do so. The approach had served him well for 28 years at Wentworth. In 1954, he addressed the topic in a speech to the United States Information Service in Karachi, Pakistan:

"One of the great difficulties which had to be overcome in America, and similarly will have to be overcome in the future in Pakistan, is the exaggerated emphasis and importance that is given to the value of a degree or degrees, especially in the industrial and technical development of the country.

"It is a wonderful ambition for a young man or woman to have, to work for a professional degree in many fields of endeavor, but there are some fields in which practical experience plus some concentrated technical training is just as valuable and this is now being recognized in America.

OF THE 654 STUDENTS ENROLLED IN DAY COURSES IN 1925-26, 359 WERE HIGH SCHOOL GRADUATES. NOT UNTIL 1930 DID WENTWORTH REQUIRE APPLICANTS FOR ADMISSION TO HOLD A HIGH SCHOOL DIPLOMA.

"Many of the most successful Americans in the last half century were not college graduates with degrees. So, although I would be the last to advocate any lessening on the part of those who have an ambition to become professional in their careers, I believe that the industrial growth of Pakistan can be speeded up considerably if good, sound practical training and experience is substituted for too many years in college."

DOBBS AND WATSON

No president or principal has enjoyed carte blanche privileges while running Wentworth. As is the case at virtually every institution of higher education, the leader of the Institute is accountable to a board of trustees. Of the five men who have led Wentworth during the past 100 years, however, Frederick Dobbs received the least leeway. The board to which he reported was anything but laissez-faire.

Paul Barron Watson, treasurer and founding director, set the tone. He was, in effect, a shadow president of the Institute during most of the Dobbs era. He was as hands-on as a trustee gets; from his State Street office he kept daily watch over the school that his former client and friend had founded at the turn of the century. Nothing, big or small, escaped his notice. Watson constantly dashed off notes to "Mr. Dobbs" on topics as varied as a patch of brown grass on the front lawn, to enrollment or the operating budget. Mr. Watson paid frequent visits to the campus. Each time he did, Principal Dobbs made sure to scurry outside and greet (or intercept) the treasurer as he strode up the walkway to the Main Building.

Somehow, their relationship seemed to work. No record exists of either man being displeased with the other's performance. Watson certainly had cause to be happy with Dobbs. Although the Institute did not grow remarkably during the Dobbs years, it did hit a nice stride under the principal's direction.

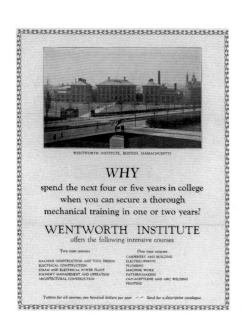

Above: The rhetorical question posed in this 1928 advertisement illustrates the niche into which Wentworth Institute had settled quite comfortably. Wentworth was an appealing destination for young men interested in entering industry quickly and productively.

Right: A typical correspondence from Treasurer Paul Watson to Principal Frederick Dobbs. Despite his office being four miles away in downtown Boston, Watson paid fierce attention to the state of affairs at the Wentworth campus.

The two most significant building projects undertaken in the Dobbs era.

Above: A 1926 rendering of the Auditorium Building (today called Watson Hall). The architects were Kilham, Hopkins & Greeley of Boston.

Above right: The 1941 construction of the building that is today called Rubenstein Hall. The main floor of this building was used as a gymnasium for many years. Its parquet floor of herringbone design was just barely large enough to house a basketball court (so long as you didn't mind risking a broken nose on full-speed layups). The basement level was originally intended as a field house, but the onset of the Second World War changed those plans. Instead, it accommodated diesel engine shops, a crucial component of the Institute's military training initiatives.

In 1924, the year Dobbs took charge of Wentworth Institute, 618 day students enrolled at a school offering 15 programs. When he left in 1952—despite the impact of the Great Depression and World War II—enrollment had stayed steady at 569 day students and 12 programs were in place.

Frederick Dobbs was a capable builder, if not an eager one. Economic and geo-political crises conspired with the principal's stay-the-course instincts to yield less building activity at the Institute than one might expect during a span of 28 years. Watson Hall (1927), Rubenstein Hall (1941), and Kingman Hall (1945) were built on Dobbs' watch. The first of these facilities received particular acclaim; home of the school auditorium and, for many years, the cafeteria, Watson Hall remains to this day the most graceful building on Wentworth's campus.

SUPPLY AND DEMAND

Of the five men who've led Wentworth, Dobbs was the only one to have taught at the Institute as well. This experience likely contributed to his keen management of the school's curriculum.

Educational philosophies have remained unalloyed throughout the Institute's lifetime. On a nuts-and-bolts level, however, Wentworth has always needed to sustain an uncommon vigilance with its curricular offerings. A liberal arts college will always have English or Philosophy or Economics in its catalog. Wentworth, on the other hand, has always had to keep its ear close to the ground in crafting its curriculum. The Institute never subscribed to the idea of education for educa-

---

IN THE 1924-25 SCHOOL YEAR:

Number of graduates interviewed for employment positions	550
Number of positions filled through efforts of Institute Employment Bureau	333
Number of direct requests received from employers for Wentworth graduates	110
Number of Wentworth men out of employment	3

—Tekton, Summer 1925

tion's sake; its stance from day one was unfailingly practical. Supply and demand has always guided decision making at Wentworth. The day, for instance, that industry ceased to require a critical mass of steam and diesel engineers was the same day the major stopped being offered at Wentworth.

Dobbs and the trustees managed this process nimbly. For example, the Institute had offered a printing program since 1917. By the early 1940s, however, Wentworth's administration realized that job openings in the trade were drying up. Printing had evolved into one of the most nepotistic industries in the Northeast, greatly diminishing a non-relative's chances of advancing on merit. As a result, when Wentworth reopened in 1946 after its World War II hiatus, the Printing Department had disappeared.

Advances in technology also contributed to revamped curricula. In 1935, the Institute finally scrapped the one-year day courses that had been offered since 1911. The reason? One year no longer afforded enough time to teach all the necessary skills in disciplines—such as machine work or pattern making—that had grown more and more complex. So, Dobbs bumped these majors up to two-year programs; others, such as plumbing or masonry and plastering, he terminated.

For every program that died off, a new two-year offering tended to rise in its place. One that began in 1932 was aircraft construction and design, hardly an easy program to initiate in the midst of the Great Depression. But Wentworth's administration saw opportunity when they looked at an aircraft industry that was expanding substantially. The program became a success; more than 700 men graduated from it during the next 32 years.

Below right: The electrical installation and maintenance laboratory, 1930. The lab was located in the basement of the Main Building.

Below: Some samples produced by Edward B. Cundall, a 1924 graduate of the printing program. The piece at lower left is a dance card, with the original pencil still bound in place.

Regardless of what was being taught, difficulties persisted in keeping the Institute properly staffed and equipped, especially during the Depression years. In 1932, Wentworth's tuition for day courses was $150. Yet, it cost an estimated $400 a year to educate each student.

This gap often turned the process of budgeting for operational and capital expenses into an ordeal. And the frequent, rapid changes that occurred in the disciplines taught by Wentworth only magnified the problem.

A visiting committee toured Wentworth Institute in 1935. Among its findings:

- In the steam and power laboratory, Mr. Edwards "was paralyzed by indecision;" he was unsure whether to direct his department's budget toward courses in refrigeration or diesel. Conflicting evidence on the trend of each field made it a high-stakes choice for the department head.
- In the welding laboratory, Mr. Tapp "felt that his department needs five more electric welding machines very badly."
- In the machine shop, the aging equipment gave the committee members pause: "In this department the same thing holds true as with a great many of the other departments; that is, the obsolescence of the machinery. A great deal of the equipment is what was originally put into the department when the school was built more than 20 years ago."

At the end of their visit, the committee members stopped by to discuss their findings with Principal Dobbs. He appeared "very much interested in the criticisms that we mentioned to him, although he was somewhat at a loss to know what to do about some of them, due to the failure of the board of directors to appropriate the necessary funds to correct some of these."

These challenges notwithstanding, the Institute remained solvent through the 1930s and into the early '40s. Because tuition stayed so low at the Institute, day enrollments didn't slack off as dramatically during the Depression years as they had at other colleges.

Machine shop, 1930. Today, the space is home to the Student Services Center on the first floor of Williston Hall.

Above: A 1932 commencement booklet, printed by Institute students. The artwork is quintessential Wentworth: How do you pull yourself out of the Great Depression? Well, you grab a trowel and some blueprints, and you get the hell to work. Now, that's the Wentworth Way!

Above right: The 46 able instructors who made up the faculty of Wentworth Institute in 1928. Seven men in the photo were honored in 1968 by having buildings officially dedicated in their names. Five of them sit side-by-side in the front row, starting third from left: John Mickelson, Frank Willson, Frederick Dobbs, Leigh Rodgers, and William Edwards. The other honorees were Chester Tudbury, second row, leftmost; and Edward Kingman, back row, third from right.

Whatever losses occurred in day enrollments, the Institute's evening school made up for them. Evening school had been a winner for Wentworth since 1911. Wentworth Institute always believed fiercely in furthering the education (or, to borrow a phrase popular in 1911, "contributing to the betterment") of the working man. The Institute knew how to market these courses to both the employer and the employee, as demonstrated in a line from its 1925 catalog: "Evening courses are planned to increase efficiency in present occupations or to aid in securing promotions."

In the late '20s, Wentworth changed the name of its evening operation to the "School of Mechanics." It offered courses such as electric wiring or forging and welding, for $20 each. Men met two hours per night, three times a week. The new name was Watson's brainchild: "We have in the past suffered somewhat from being known as a trade school," he wrote. "We do not teach people how to trade—we leave that to Wall Street. We simply teach mechanics; and that people may get a clear conception of our work we ought to call our institution a school of mechanics." As it turned out, the name lasted for only a decade.

In addition to providing the Institute a steady, reliable source of income, evening school also served a valuable public relations role for Wentworth. It demonstrated to the school's core constituents—the working man, the trades-man, the laborer—that this was a place that cared about their well-being, and that delivered educational services important to them.

The short-lived logo of Wentworth Institute's School of Mechanics.

The Ballad of a Commuter

by William A. Downing, C&B '29

Each morning I hop an express
To go into Boston and school,
Some days I forget my ticket
And naturally feel like a fool.

When the train gets into South Station
I look 'round with a nonchalant air,
And realize that I must be moving
Because we are just about there.

As I rise to my feet in a hurry
And swing down off the car,
I comfort myself with the cheerful thought
That the subway is not far.

I plunge down into the tunnel
And get a subway train,
I join the army of strap-hangers
And start to get profane.

I hold my breath at Park Street
And rush on up the stairs,
To a bedlam of noise and tumult,
And of conductors shouting, "Fares!"

Finally my car comes rumbling along
Clanging its strident bell,
But then the mob gets awful
And I have to push like H___!

Just as I start to climb in,
The porter shuts the door.
It's probably his idea of sport,
But it gets me good and sore.

So back into the mob I go once more
To wrestle with school girls and men,
And to wait for a Huntington Avenue car
Which comes about once in ten.

At last I succeed in getting aboard.
A fact which me does amaze,
And not till we pass the Copley
Do I start to come out of my daze.

We pass along the avenue
With many stops and starts
And I breathe a sigh of relief when we finally reach
The Boston Museum of Arts.

I get out there and cross the street
And go into my school,
Wentworth by name, long live its fame!
As an exponent of the tool.

You are welcome, my reader, to finish this poem
If you want to waste your time.
As for me, I'm going to "hit the hay"
And seek the sandman's clime.

A classic view of Wentworth Institute, looking across from the Museum of Fine Arts. The brick memorial to Arioch Wentworth is visible on Huntington Avenue. It remained there until the '60s, when the city claimed land from Wentworth in order to widen the street. Today, the brick pillars on the fence around Sweeney Field pay homage to this heritage.

ANNUAL
BASEBALL GAME
Wentworth vs. Phillips Andover
Wed., April 29, 1925   at 2:30 P. M.
ROUND TRIP TICKET $1.20
(Transportation by Auto)

ONE ADMISSION
BASEBALL GAME
PHILLIPS ANDOVER
VS.
WENTWORTH
April 29, 1925   50 cents

The sporting life during the Dobbs era.

Above: The Power Plant's smokestack offers an inviting target to Wentworth batter John Goumas in a 1947 home contest against the Boston University freshman team.

Top right: The 1937 rifle team; riflery is the second oldest sport at Wentworth. The team's home base has varied through the years. For 40 years, the firing range lived in the loft of the West Building (Williston Hall); in 1957, it moved to the subterranean level of the East Building (Dobbs Hall). Since 1970, however, a first-class firing range has operated on the bottom floor of the Nelson Recreation Center.

Above right: A hot ticket on campus during the spring of 1925.

Right: The intramural basketball team of 1926 machine work students. The players' incongruous uniforms are a bit puzzling. Above the waist, the men are clearly ready for roundball. Below, however, they appear poised for a formal business meeting.

13. Luther H. Blount, MC&TD '37
The Inventor

For decades, Luther Blount has been a tough-minded nautical entrepreneur. It all began at Wentworth, where he earned a machine construction and tool design certificate in 1937. After Wentworth, he spent six years as a plant manager at Belding Hemingway Corricelli. Upon returning from World War II, he went to work in the family oyster business in Rhode Island. In 1949, he designed and built his first oyster boat, a success that prompted him to launch his own boatbuilding company, Blount Marine Corporation, in Warren, R.I. During the next 50 years, he built all kinds of boats: ferries, tugs, oil exploration vessels, and floating hospitals. His forte, passenger cruisers, led him to found the American Canadian Caribbean Line in 1969. As a boatbuilder and a businessman, Blount has always relied on his own devices, literally and figuratively. He is an unparalleled inventor, with more than 40 patents to his name. They include advances such as the bow boarding ramp and the pint-a-flush toilet. "Everything you see on my boats," says Blount, "can be traced back to what I learned as an MC&TD student at Wentworth."

14. Frederick E. Dobbs
The Principal

Frederick Dobbs led Wentworth for 28 years, a full decade longer than any other principal or president. From 1924 to 1952, he served as the Institute's second principal, leading it through a Great Depression and a World War. He was an able administrator—not flashy but steadfast, not dynamic but productive. When Wentworth Institute opened its doors in 1911, the 28-year-old Dobbs was on staff as a teacher of applied sciences. When wartime training began at the Institute six years later, he took a leading role in implementing the programs. This caught the eye of Principal Arthur Williston, who soon made Dobbs his assistant. After Williston resigned in 1923, the directors unanimously chose Dobbs to replace him as principal. His primary interest was keeping Wentworth Institute relevant. He oversaw the school with the mindset of a manufacturer. It all boiled down to supply and demand in Dobbs' eyes: when the need for printing tradesmen started to diminish in the '40s, Dobbs axed the program without hesitation. When a resurgent economy sparked a home construction boom, Dobbs speedily introduced a building construction major to fit the times. He showed strong leadership during the difficult years of World War II. The principal strongly advocated that the school shut down to dedicate its facilities and faculty to U.S. Navy training efforts. In the early '50s, the Ford Foundation asked Dobbs to develop technical schools in Pakistan based on the Wentworth model. He resigned from Wentworth in 1952; three years later, he received the James H. McGraw Award from the American Society for Engineering Education.

15. Benjamin Garfink, MC&TD '14
The Chef

Among the first students who walked through the halls of Wentworth Institute in 1911 was a young man named Ben Garfink. After graduating in 1914, he ran the lunchroom (Ben's Café) at Wentworth for an astounding 53 years. No one,

including Ben himself, ever claimed he was a master chef. Alumni joked, for instance, that his all-purpose gravy could be used to glue the soles of shoes to the uppers. But slinging chow for half a century undersells Garfink's accomplishments. More important, he served as advisor, helper, confidant, and booster to three generations of Wentworth men. "Ben helped more young men through this school than anyone but Arioch Wentworth," says Charlie Pheeney, EC '48. Upon retiring in 1967, Garfink bequeathed to his alma mater an endowment that made possible the presentation of the Babcock Scholarship to deserving students. After decades of filling students' bellies, how fitting that Ben took it upon himself to nourish the academic ambitions of future generations of Wentworth pupils.

16. Franklin W. Hobbs
The Industrialist

Wentworth has been fortunate to be led by many able board chairmen. Franklin W. Hobbs, an MIT graduate, belongs in the upper tier of that select group. A member of the Institute's board of directors since 1926, Hobbs rose to the chairmanship in 1940, a time when firm leadership was never

more needed. Together with Principal Frederick Dobbs, Chairman Hobbs steered the Institute through the war years, including a two-year enrollment hiatus, and positioned the school to thrive in the postwar environment. Hobbs brought an insider's awareness to his guidance of Wentworth Institute. He was one of New England's foremost industrialists; from 1913 to his death in 1955, he headed Arlington Mills, a huge textile manufacturing plant in Lawrence, Mass.

17. James M. Morton Jr.
The Judge

The Honorable James Madison Morton chaired Wentworth's board of directors from 1922 until his death in 1940, the second-longest tenure in school history. The third consecutive Harvard-educated board chairman, Morton was notewor-

thy for his sturdy leadership. He and Principal Frederick Dobbs enjoyed a close working relationship. A lifelong resident of Fall River, Mass., Morton was the son of a Massachusetts Supreme Court justice. He followed his father's footsteps in 1912 when President William Taft appointed him as a judge in the U.S. District Court for Massachusetts. President Herbert Hoover later promoted him to the U.S. Circuit Court in 1931.

18. C. Wesley Nelson
The Educator

Toward the end of his 41-year career at Wentworth, peers used the phrase, "master teacher," time and again to describe C. Wesley Nelson. He was that and more. Nelson joined the faculty in 1928 as an instructor in the Steam and Diesel Engineering Department. For the next 30 years,

he was regarded as one of the Institute's finest educators. Moreover, he developed into a leading authority on refrigeration; his text, *Commercial and Industrial Refrigeration* became the gold standard in the field. In

1958, President Beatty moved Nelson into the administrative ranks; he served as dean of instruction until his retirement in 1969. "He was a lovely man," says Professor Ray Tavares, who was hired by Nelson in 1962. "He was rigid, so you had to get to know him to find out how caring he really was. He took good care of the faculty. He was always proud, well-dressed, and a good family man; a good person to look up to." Howard Wetzell, S&DE '51, ran into Dean Nelson 35 years after graduating: "We had a great conversation. He was still interested in me after all those years. A wonderful human being." In 1971, Wentworth named its Recreation Center after Dean Nelson.

19. Chester W. Tudbury
The Righthand Man

Of the five men who have led Wentworth during its first 100 years, Frederick Dobbs served the longest. His lieutenant, Chester Tudbury, contributed mightily to that distinction. For three decades a loyal assistant to Dobbs, Tudbury did

much of the heavy lifting in the academic arena, a service that helped guarantee his boss' longevity. A high school principal before he joined the Institute in 1918 as a mathematics instructor, Tudbury was described as "a beloved teacher who molded the character of his students while imparting knowledge." As an administrator, he especially enjoyed the supervisor of instruction role. He was a caring advocate for Wentworth faculty members. When Principal Dobbs informed the board in 1952 that he would not return from his sabbatical, Tudbury argued vigorously against replacing him with Acting Principal Marshall Arlin. The reason, he told the directors, was that the faculty held Arlin in low regard. In his opinion, there existed three superior in-house choices: Joe Tansey, Wesley Nelson, or Harold Rice. The directors paid attention to Tudbury's negative recommendation, if not his positive ones. They opened a search and ultimately gave the job to an outsider from Pratt Institute, H. Russell Beatty. And if Tudbury played even a small role in making that happen, then he is an important figure in Wentworth's history.

"WORKING FOR A LIVING"

June 8, 1933

Dear George (Pierce),

In reply to yours of the 5th, I shall try to be present for the 20th anniversary of our graduation from Wentworth Institute. I have had quite a little time off from my work of late. I buried my father the 18th of May and before his death, transported him to and from hospitals in Boston.

My employer might get sore and use this time off as an excuse for a ride. For the last year and a half, I have been working 36 hours a week. The work is not what it used to be. Just a job now.

Of course, I feel thankful that I have a job. There were only a few of us that were put on short hours. We are on just substation maintenance work now.

If I am not present and anyone asks for me, tell them I am still working for a living and still believe in Honesty-Energy-Economy-System, which is practiced by very few today.

Classmate of 20 years ago,

Forrest L. Turner, MC&TD '13

[George Pierce, a 1913 electrical construction and operation graduate, was registrar of Wentworth Institute for many years.]

TODAY'S FAIRY TALE

"Once there was a Wentworth student who *never* lit his cigarette upon the front steps, who *never* slid in the corridors, who *never* crowded the Simmons girls away from the street car, who *never* copied a bit of homework, who *never* threw an eraser, who *never* sang in the hallways, and who *never* raced up and down Huntington Avenue in his car."

—Tekton, April 1929

AUTOMOBILES

Students are not permitted to drive off of the Institute grounds during the noon recess.

FREDERICK E. DOBBS
Principal

SUCCEEDING FROM SCRATCH

by Willard B. Merrill, MC&TD '37

A New Hampshire boy, born in 1914. Graduated from high school in 1932 in the middle of the Great Depression. I had very little money for college. No jobs available. How unlucky can you be?

So, back to high school where I took a fifth year of mechanical drafting, advanced math, and typing. I was very interested in working with my hands, mechanical projects and woodworking. Built a beautiful boat in my basement for less than twelve dollars. Mowed lawns, shoveled snow, and finally got my first real job in a shoe shop—dirty, noisy, and dangerous business. Worked almost two years cutting heavy leather without any mishaps.

At last with finances, the happiest, most excited young man in the state boarded a bus from Portsmouth, N.H., headed for Boston. I was excited to be on my own. Excited about the upcoming life in the big city and excited about being an accepted student at Wentworth. It was registration day.

The big city was new to me. I purposely walked from the bus station almost the entire length of Huntington Avenue towards the school just to savor the day. I was whistling, skipping, and looking up as I studied the tall buildings. Approaching Wentworth, I first climbed the stairs of the Museum of Fine Arts and in the company of the Indian I spent a few minutes gazing across the avenue enjoying the view of Wentworth and its surroundings. The school would be my home away from home for the next two years.

From that September day in 1935, everything has been uphill. I remember the first day in drafting class, how green my classmates were. They were strange to drawing boards, drafting instruments, and slide rules. One fellow holding up his T-square asked me, "What do you do with this thing?" My answer: "Use it like a hammer to pound in the thumb tacks." That same fellow graduated and went on to become a most successful entrepreneur. Typically that year, machine construction and tool design scholars made the best investments of their lives.

Since graduation I have never looked back. Worked with well-known corporations. My designs made millions. I was in business with top engineers. Enjoyed my relationship with laborers and professional personnel alike, all the time wearing proudly my Wentworth heritage.

Enjoyed many business trips with men in industry. I recall one in particular with a banker. We were relaxing at the end of a busy day, playing chess. "Bill," he said, "you have never talked much about your schooling." My response: "I graduated from Wentworth Institute in 1937. Checkmate."

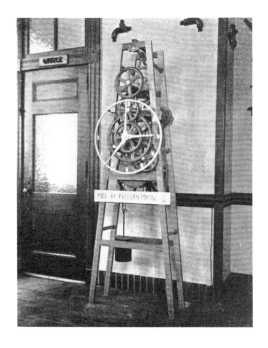

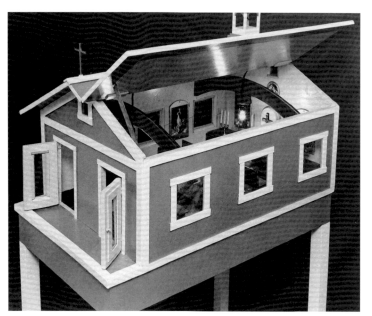

Idle hands were never much of a concern at Wentworth Institute.

Above: A 1932 example of the annual project for the pattern making class. "This clock is made of pine, mahogany, maple, and hickory," described the 1932 Wentworth Alumni News, "and contains 17 gears and pinions, a metal pendulum, and is weighted by a 100-pound cylinder. It is complete in every detail, having hour, minute, and second hands, which are on one main shaft in the center of a 24-inch dial. Every movement of the mechanism can be seen doing its part toward keeping that perfect Wentworth Time!"

Above right: A church model crafted by a 1950 building construction student.

Right: Another shop exercise of pattern making students; this one a 1940 wooden cutaway of a steam engine.

WORLD WAR II

The Second World War sent a shockwave through Wentworth Institute.

Recalling the fine service Wentworth had provided to the national cause 25 years earlier, the U.S. government was quick to seek the Institute's help once again. Less than three months after Japan's attack on Pearl Harbor, the War Department contacted Wentworth Institute and asked it to run the Naval Training School. Principal Dobbs was well suited to head the effort; he had been Arthur Williston's righthand man during the Institute's training of World War I recruits.

The government's request didn't come out of the blue. As the War in Europe escalated in the late 1930s, Wentworth had been chosen to administer a couple of less intense military training initiatives. From 1939 to 1941, Wentworth and the New England Aircraft School trained 2,500 mechanics for the Army Air Force. And from 1940 to 1942, Massachusetts War Industries sent about 5,000 students to the Institute for brief technical instruction.

The Naval Training School, by contrast, was a full-fledged training program. Instruction began on May 15, 1942. Because Wentworth had remained open for normal business during its World War I training, it attempted to do so again with the NTS. As a result, the 1942-43 school year saw Wentworth Institute burn its instructional candle at both ends.

For the first four months, the Navy recruits had the Institute to themselves. Then, in September 1942, Wentworth students arrived on campus to begin their school year. They quickly learned to identify themselves as "civilian students," since they shared the Institute with 500 sailors. Another cohort of 500 sailors showed up for night instruction.

The Tekton Yearbook credited Principal Dobbs for the care he paid to the "regular students" that year: "Our principal was careful to see that the presence of the sailors should not, in any way, interfere with regular students receiving their usual high-grade instruction. Efforts have been made to live up to this plan and,

The second group of basic engineers who completed the Naval Training School program at Wentworth. Stephen "Weaser" Kustan (rear row, fifth from left), of Saint Clair, Pa., was just one of the 10,000 young men who trained at Wentworth during the war years. After finishing at Wentworth in early 1944, Kustan was a gunner assigned to the LSM-36 landing craft in the Pacific Theater. During his service, he earned a Purple Heart along with a dozen other medals and commendations.

GROUP 2 1944 N.T.S. (BASIC ENGINEERS)
WENTWORTH INSTITUTE BOSTON, MASS.

A CENTURY OF HONESTY, ENERGY, ECONOMY, SYSTEM

The Hotel Somerset in Kenmore Square offered lodging for the participants in the Naval Training School.

although there were many times when the school could have been run more economically by combining the classes, as numbers had diminished because of the draft, very few such combinations were made. In spite of the fact that the average class dropped as low as eight men, the regular teachers carried on gallantly with small classes and offered the same instruction as in the past."

Lt. Commander Frank Cavanagh of the Navy demonstrated the cooperative spirit that made this cohabitation manageable. On December 14, 1942, the Navy inspected the facilities at Wentworth to see how the recruits, and the Institute, were faring. Cavanagh reported to Principal Dobbs: "The corridor adjacent to the mess hall was quite dirty. I realize that your school has a sufficient number of janitors to keep this corridor as clean as other parts of the building but because of the fact that it is constantly in use by naval personnel, Lt. Anderson, Educational Officer, has been instructed if and when the floor is again dirty that he is to detail several sailors to sweep the premises. It is the Navy's dirt, therefore I hope you will have no objection to the Navy cleaning it."

The machinist's mate insignia. Endicott Peabody, governor of Massachusetts from 1963 to 1965, was a notable graduate of Wentworth's Naval Training School.

This cooperation notwithstanding, when the civilian students went home in May 1943, the trustees and Principal Dobbs decided to focus the Institute's efforts solely on operating the Naval Training School. For the first and only time in its history, Wentworth Institute shut down its normal operations. It spent the next two years wholly in the service of the federal government.

During the First World War, the recruits had pitched tents on campus, creating Camp Wentworth. With the Naval Training School, however, the Institute acted as a commuter school for the trainees. Naval recruits bunked in the Hotel Somerset on Commonwealth Avenue in Kenmore Square; each morning after reveille they marched a mile to Wentworth, where they spent a long day receiving technical training.

NAVAL TRAINING SCHOOL
Machinist's Mate

WENTWORTH INSTITUTE
Boston, Massachusetts

More than 10,000 men completed the program. A new group of 100 men arrived each week to begin the intensive eight-week regimen under the tutelage of Wentworth instructors. The course of study was rigidly formulated to meet the requirements set forth by the Navy; it consisted of mathematics, drawing, power plant practice, motor laboratory work, and machine shop practice. Upon completing their studies, the men were qualified as Navy machinist's mates, first class, and basic engineers. The NTS also graduated 700 metalsmiths.

Navy machinist's mates learn the ins and outs of operating steam and electrical machinery, 1944.

The Naval Training School ended on October 10, 1944. The Navy rated Wentworth Institute the best of any contract school in the country for the training of enlisted engineers (machinist's mates, diesel engineers, and metal-smiths). In fact, the Navy kept Wentworth under contract longer than any other school of its type.

Many graduates of the Naval Training School acquired a taste for Wentworth. After completing their tours of duty, nearly 50 of these men enrolled at Wentworth Institute as full-time students in 1946 and 1947.

Wentworth was connected to the war effort in other ways, too, of course. The Institute estimated that 1,500 of its graduates fought in World War II. Forty-eight of them died in action. [*See list at right.*]

Wilfred G. Holsberg, S&DE '39, of Winthrop, Mass., exemplified the bravery displayed by each of these 1,500 veterans. The 24-year-old Lieutenant Holsberg shipped overseas in 1943 and spent five months in the European Theater of Operations. He took part in the fighting at Anzio and the bombing of Rome. On March 17, 1944, he was the navigator of a B-17 aircraft in a bombing mission over Toulon, France.

Lieutenant Wilfred G. Holsberg's 1939 graduation photo.

That night, enemy aircraft engaged the plane and gunfire ripped through both of Lt. Holsberg's legs. Despite the intense pain of these wounds, Holsberg dragged himself over to the bombardier, who was dazed, and revived his comrade in time for him to release the bombs on their target. As the damaged plane returned home, it was forced to leave formation and fly at a low level. Clinging to consciousness through sheer strength of will, Holsberg successfully navigated his crew back to the base. Both his legs were later amputated. Lt. Wilfred Holsberg was awarded the Distinguished Service Cross for heroism on September 18, 1944.

Navy recruits salute the flag during a ceremony to mark the Naval Training School's last day of operation on October 10, 1944.

A memorial, dedicated in 1994, honoring the 48 Wentworth alumni who died in World War II fighting.

WENTWORTH ALUMNI WHO DIED SERVING IN WORLD WAR II

"To honor these men of Wentworth, Their sacrifice shall be our inspiration"

Lawrence C. Archer '24

Karl H. Bardwell '35

Phillips Bradley '40

Roland L. Bumpus '40

Graham B. Cameron '36

Everett Carney '27

John F. Crawford '31

Henry J. Downs '34

William H. Emhardt '38

Donald C. Farwell '43

Warren A. Fenno '40

Milton J. Fine '42

Francis C. Gonsalves '37

Roland M. Gray '43

Merrill A. Green '36

Edward J. Gusiora '41

George Henneberry '43

Theodore M. Jackson '39

George H. Jordan '42

Anthony Kesishian '40

Howard L. Lewis '43

Robert W. Lougee '43

John W. May '41

George McAdams '39

Richard Q. McLean '42

Suren Melkonian '39

Richard T. Merrill '34

Carlos G. Millett '21

Fred Mitchell '39

Robert L. Moore '42

John R. Patch '34

Edmond F. Potter '42

Frederick S. Raftery '39

Richard F. Readel '42

Clyde F. Reeves '41

Miner B. Robinson '33

Charles J. Russala '41

Howard C. Shaw '43

Stanley H. Smith '39

Newton D. Stanley '35

Otto M. Theurer '31

James M. Tobin '43

John V. Travers '43

C. Sumner Walker '43

Franklin S. Wescott '41

George S. Wheeler '39

Harold P. Wood '39

Thomas R. Yates '40

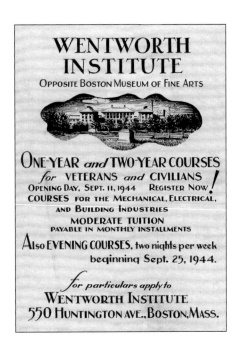

WENTWORTH
INSTITUTE
OPPOSITE BOSTON MUSEUM OF FINE ARTS

ONE-YEAR *and* TWO-YEAR COURSES
for VETERANS *and* CIVILIANS !
OPENING DAY, SEPT. 11, 1944   REGISTER NOW !
COURSES FOR THE MECHANICAL, ELECTRICAL,
AND BUILDING INDUSTRIES
MODERATE TUITION
PAYABLE IN MONTHLY INSTALLMENTS
ALSO EVENING COURSES, two nights per week
beginning Sept. 25, 1944.

for particulars apply to
WENTWORTH INSTITUTE
550 HUNTINGTON AVE., BOSTON, MASS.

Above: Originally, Wentworth administrators intended the school to shut down for only one year. This flier, printed in September 1944, reflected that optimistic plan. Shortly after its publication, however, Institute trustees decided that the school needed another full year to "reconvert" to civilian instruction.

Below: The new electronics laboratory on the second floor of the East Building, 1948. The lab featured 24 work benches, procured courtesy of postwar surplus programs.

BACK TO THE BUSINESS OF TEACHING

In the spring of 1945, Principal Dobbs steered the Institute through a yearlong process he called "reconversion." Laboratories that had been overhauled to suit the needs of the Naval Training School were now reconfigured once more to accommodate the needs of 300 first-year day students (two-thirds of whom were World War II veterans) and 400 evening students.

When classes finally reopened on January 28, 1946, the Institute's classrooms and labs looked quite different than they had in the spring of 1943. Taking advantage of postwar surplus programs, Wentworth upgraded its equipment with great success. The machine shop added three milling machines, three grinders, two lathes, and a harness tester. The welding shop now featured a spot welder and an atomic hydrogen welder. The diesel lab picked up a handful of three- and four-cylinder diesel engines for students to cut their teeth on. The second floor of the East Building (today Dobbs Hall) welcomed a new electronics laboratory. And a new building (known today as Kingman Hall) for aircraft instruction took shape, complete with first-rate furnishings (four surplus airplanes as well as 13 aircraft engines).

One of the era's finest and most enduring national legacies was the establishment of the GI Bill. Enacted in 1944, the law subsidized the college education of hundreds of thousands of veterans. Wentworth Institute welcomed back the GIs enthusiastically. From 1946 to about 1954, the bill helped create an interesting mix of men in Wentworth classrooms. For instance, 26 men enrolled in the architectural construction program in September 1946. Six fresh-faced 18-year-olds had the good fortune to study alongside 20 battle-hardened veterans of World War II. Among these 20 GIs, eleven were married and seven were fathers. It's a safe bet that the six 18-year-olds learned a good deal more than how to frame a house during their two years at Wentworth Institute.

While Wentworth welcomed the GI Bill with open arms, it held a different opinion of the federal government's draft policies. The Selective Service System administered the mandatory draft of able-bodied young men into the armed services. From June 1950 to June 1953, Uncle Sam inducted 1.5 million young men to serve in the Korean War.

The law stated that "drafted students attending colleges, universities, or similar institutions of learning, shall be permitted to remain in their classes until the end of the academic year." Regrettably, however, most Wentworth students drafted in the early 1950s were not granted that privilege. The government, it turns out, did not classify Wentworth Institute in the same category as a college or university.

This policy infuriated Principal Dobbs. He sent nonstop letters and telegrams to congressmen, Cabinet members, and generals. In October 1951, for instance, he detailed his argument to General Lewis Hershey, who headed the Selective

Found on the Bulletin Board

U.S.S. Wentworth Institute

To: All hands
From: Executive Officer
Subject: Recreation

In keeping with the ship's policy of allowing the crew to participate in all forms of recreation that they desire, the following item from the Boston Post has been brought to my attention:

Seek Quota at Simmons

Simmons wives, graduate and undergraduate, are failing to do their part in increasing the nation's population, according to an article in the February issue of the Simmons Review alumnae publication. Simmons wives were asked by the Review to help increase the number of intelligent leaders to guide the country and to aid in the replenishment of the diminishing birth rate among college graduates.

All hands who are interested in rectifying the above situation shall muster at 13:30, Friday 21, in front of the Administration Building at Simmons College in undressed mattress covers and watch caps. Shoes or sneakers are optional.

R.E. Schmalz, Executive Officer

Copies to all compartments

——Wentworth Alumni Quarterly, April 1947

Above: A lighthearted moment in the electrical construction laboratory, 1951.

Top: Before the mid-1950s, Wentworth owned no dormitories, which meant that students from distant locales had to secure housing on their own. Here, two friends from the Class of 1942 hit the books in their small apartment on Saint Botolph Street.

A building construction class project, 1947.

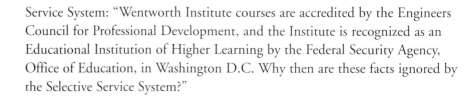

Service System: "Wentworth Institute courses are accredited by the Engineers Council for Professional Development, and the Institute is recognized as an Educational Institution of Higher Learning by the Federal Security Agency, Office of Education, in Washington D.C. Why then are these facts ignored by the Selective Service System?"

Marshall Arlin, acting principal from 1952 to 1953.

Principal Dobbs also protested to U.S. Secretary of Labor Maurice Tobin, who was sympathetic but ultimately unhelpful: "The students who are drafted," wrote Dobbs, "are especially bitter because they know, or learn, of others attending art schools, music schools, business schools, etc., who are deferred without question, and they can't understand the difference."

Dobbs and Wentworth Institute did not win the appeal. Not until the 1960s did the school finally earn from the government the status of a "similar institution of learning."

After 28 years as principal, Frederick Dobbs took a sabbatical from the Institute in 1951, and within a year he submitted his resignation to the board. In his place, the trustees appointed instructor Marshall Arlin to serve as acting principal. He served a year, during which time his rapport with the faculty worsened by the day. Consequently, the trustees chose to look outside Wentworth for a full-time replacement for Dobbs. They found their man at the same place at which Williston had worked and Dobbs had studied: Pratt Institute.

AIR FORCE CONTRACTS

In 1946, a venture known as Air Force Contracts began. Wentworth has always been a teaching institution; seldom has research been more than an afterthought for faculty. Air Force Contracts stands as a notable exception in the school's history.

In the years following World War II, the armed services started to spend serious money on R&D. In 1946, Dr. Marcus O'Day of the Cambridge Research Laboratories approached Wentworth seeking support for an upper air research project on which he was working for the U.S. Department of Defense. At O'Day's request, Wentworth instructors instrumented two V-2 rockets that the U.S. had confiscated in Germany during the war.

Wentworth's work on the project impressed the U.S. Air Force. In short time, the USAF selected the Institute to carry out some of its research projects on a contract basis. Wentworth was the only technical institute in the country accorded that privilege. Year after year, separate from their teaching responsibilities, Wentworth faculty members worked in an Institute laboratory on projects that included fabricating the payloads and instrumentation of rockets and test balloons. It was an active operation; between 1950 and 1953, for instance, Wentworth Institute completed 177 projects for the Air Force.

A 1956 newspaper article described the lab's reputation for precision: "As you can imagine, building the complicated electronics equipment to go in rocket heads is a very precise job. Build one off center, or just a little bit out of balance, and it will wobble and probably crash. Get just one of a vast number of wires connected wrong and the electronic equipment won't function. All you have succeeded in doing is shooting taxpayers' money into the stratosphere. But thanks to the skilled craftsmanship at Wentworth, this sort of thing doesn't happen."

For 50 years, with little fanfare, the Institute maintained this laboratory. For many years, the Air Force was the sole client. In later years, as other government clients such as NASA contracted with the Institute, the name was changed to Wentworth Laboratories. Working with a dedicated staff (although faculty members still consulted as needed) on the third floor of Williston Hall, Wentworth Labs averaged more than a million dollars of contracted business each year until it was shut down in 1997.

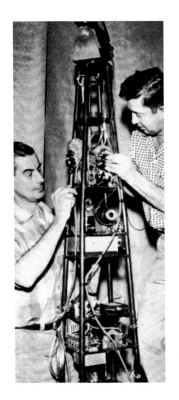

Left: Air Force Contracts employees Frank Cleveland, left, and Ed Karpinski, MW&TM '49, wire an Aerobee rocket.

Below: The payload instrumentation and nosecone sections of the Aerobee Airglow-11 Rocket built at Wentworth.

WENTWORTH'S Football Dynasty

"Football has been added to the athletics program at Wentworth Institute and will undoubtedly become the most popular sport.... Spectators will realize that they are witnessing a battle between 22 well-trained and well-nigh perfect physical specimens of young manhood who are struggling with a maximum of effort in a game that requires strength, speed, skill, endurance, and, most of all, brains and strategy....Football is a developer of character. It requires courage, cooperation, loyalty, obedience, and self sacrifice. It develops quick thinking and cool-headedness under stress; it promotes clean living and habits; it creates self-confidence and the idea of service; and it teaches control of temper....Because of these reasons we are sure that the adoption of football as a recognized sport will prove to be a success at Wentworth Institute."

These words from the 1933 Tekton yearbook not only announced the birth of football at Wentworth, they trumpeted the arrival of a juggernaut in New England intercollegiate athletics. Though many Wentworth alumni may be unaware that the school ever fielded a team, the fact is that from 1933 until 1951, the Technicians of Wentworth Institute ran, passed, and double-reversed their way to gridiron supremacy. Today, more than 50 years after the final gun sounded, bringing to a close a golden age in Wentworth athletics, the exploits of the Wentworth football team and its colorful coach can still be relived in the annals of the record books and in the memories of the men who graced the field.

In the fall of 1933, a call went out for football recruits and 78 men, more than 15 percent of the student body, reported to the field behind the Main Building. From this pool, Coach Joseph Tansey selected the 30 most promising athletes to begin training. Marshall Birkett, AC&D '34, a tall and athletic young man from Needham, Mass., made the cut. He had never played organized football before. "That team had some really fine players," Birkett recalled in 2001. "There were All-Scholastics from Massachusetts, New Hampshire, and Maine. We had a pretty good team, all right."

1948 action on the home field in back of the Main Building. That year, Wentworth's only loss was to the Boston University freshman team, quarterbacked by local sports legend, Harry Agganis. Six years later, he began his tragically short career with the Boston Red Sox, playing first base for a year and a half before he died of a pulmonary embolism in 1955.

Pretty good indeed. On its way to achieving a perfect 5-0 record, the inaugural Wentworth squad outscored the opposition, 96-0. Dominant on both sides of the ball, the team completed 39 of 51 "forward passes," while allowing no opponent more than two first downs in a game.

"The game has changed a lot since I was there," admits Birkett, recalling an era when men wore leather helmets and played both offense and defense. "Players weren't as big as they are now. Some were pretty big, but not like you see today. They were just tough, tough guys." (Coach Tansey once described Frank Sullivan, his 139-pound defensive end, as able to "lick his weight in wildcats.") Training philosophies were a bit different back then as well. "Nobody worked out with weights," says Birkett. "We had better things to do with our time. When football season came, you just ate more."

Play-Calling Genius

Although defense was the calling card of Joe Tansey's teams, it was the coach's madcap play calling that his players remember best.

Asked about his fondest football memories, Birkett doesn't hesitate to name his coach: "Joe Tansey was a really nice guy and a great coach. He always made football fun." Birkett pauses, the mention of Tansey's name causing his thoughts to drift back to a game, play, or moment 70 years past: "I'll tell you one thing," he smiles, "Tansey could come up with the most ridiculous plays."

The coach's unorthodox play calling was the trademark of a quick-strike Wentworth offense that could score anytime from anywhere on the field. Tales abound of Wentworth confounding opponents with "double-reverses" and "delayed line spins." A favorite from Tansey's bag of tricks was the 50-yard "hook-and-ladder" play in which the quarterback threw deep downfield to a receiver who, upon making the catch, pitched the ball to a second receiver streaking up the sideline. Not to be outdone was the "reverse-forward-lateral," which started with a pitch to the halfback, who then handed off on a reverse to the split end, who proceeded to pass to a receiver downfield, who finally lateraled to a second receiver running up the side-line. Regardless of whether one considered Tansey's play calling innovative or just insane, his teams kept winning.

Wentworth racked up victories throughout the decade, culminating in a second undefeated and unscored-upon

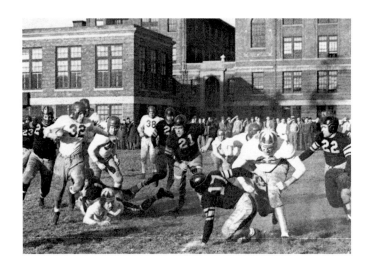

The nickname, Technicians, lasted only as long as varsity football did. For the past 50 years, Wentworth's sports teams have been known as the Leopards.

season in 1938. As the team closed out the '30s with an overall record of 28-9-3 (including an incredible 28 shutouts), they looked to the '40s with optimism. They had no way of knowing, of course, that events thousands of miles away would soon challenge the team as no opponent had yet been able to do.

The 1940 squad was built around triple-threat quarterback Bill "Vicky" Ficachello, who was the team's best passer, runner, and kicker. Come the following spring, however, the Tekton noted, "Vicky was now carrying the ball for Uncle Sam." The outbreak of World War II had changed the landscape of the whole world; Wentworth's little corner of it was no exception.

Despite more and more of its young men enlisting or being drafted into the armed forces, Wentworth still managed to field a team in 1941, and posted a 4-1-1 record. In the fall of 1942, however, Wentworth students returned to school to find themselves attending classes alongside more than 1,000 sailors. The U.S. Navy had begun sending its recruits to the Institute to receive technical training. Coach Tansey himself had left school to enlist in the Army Air Corps. The Institute canceled football, along with most other student activities, indefinitely. By 1944, the school even canceled classes, as it needed to concentrate fully on training troops. Wentworth, too, was now carrying the ball for Uncle Sam.

When the Institute reopened in 1946, it reinstated football, despite a tight budget and a diminished student population. The decision to bring back the sport responded in part to the military climate of the day: "As everyone knows," read the 1946 Tekton, "war demands that young men for the armed forces shall be fit, and men who have had contact work in sports have a heavy advantage in hand-to-hand fighting over those who have not."

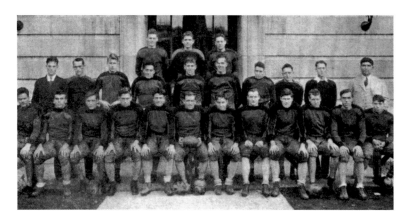

Wentworth's first football team, 1933.

The program continued for the next several years, and though the teams enjoyed success, the number of men trying out for the squad dwindled each season. The demographics of the student population had changed considerably. Many students were grown men and veterans of the war, attending Wentworth on the GI Bill. Quite a few had wives and children, leaving little time for sports.

COLD SHOWERS

As the '40s came to a close, the Wentworth Technicians continued to tackle with ease all obstacles placed before them on the playing field. Obstacles off the field, however, posed more of a challenge. The loss of tuition-paying students for two years during the war had put a financial strain on the Institute. The football program eventually began to feel the squeeze. Players made do with what little equipment was available—some wore leather helmets, others plastic. Each player had to carry his own insurance. Meal money was scarce and showers were cold. And the team no longer could afford to travel by bus. For away games, all the players piled into the cars owned by a few teammates.

"I had to hitchhike home from practice every night," recalls Peter Tsokanis, BC '52, a speedster from Brockton who starred for the Technicians during Wentworth's final two seasons. "We'd be in class from eight to four, then practice until dusk. I'd take the train to Milton and hitchhike back to Brockton in the dark. We really had to give a lot to play in those days."

Tsokanis credits his coach with making the hard work worthwhile. "Tansey was such a great guy, a real character," he recalls. "He couldn't pronounce my name so he just called me, 'Brockton.' He even gave me my own play...the Brockton play." Tsokanis explains how Tansey had him line up at halfback, then split out to the sideline with the wide receiver. On the snap the quarterback threw to Tsokanis, who in turn threw downfield to the wide receiver. Reflecting on his two years under Coach Tansey, Tsokanis' words echo those of Marshall Birkett: "Boy," he laughs, "we sure had some crazy plays."

Initially, the Institute made plans for the team to begin the 1952 season, but the lack of funds and available bodies proved too much to overcome. The school shut down the program, bringing to a close the brief but glorious history of Wentworth football. In its 15 seasons, the team had most assuredly left its print on the landscape of New England college football—posting an overall record of 53-22-12 while shutting out its opponents an astonishing 49 times.

Not only had the players achieved remarkable success, they had done it with flair, thanks to their daring, and caring, head coach. Joe Tansey remained at Wentworth until 1968, continuing to coach basketball and baseball, and serving as dean of students. Today, the gymnasium named in his honor stands on what was once Wentworth's south end zone.

As for the men who battled on the gridiron on behalf of Wentworth Institute, they established a standard of success and consistency of which the entire Wentworth community can always be proud.

Reprinted from "Gridiron Glory Days," by Robert Zagarella, Wentworth Magazine, Winter 2001.

Stars of the 1949 squad: quarterback David McKee, AC '50, left, and his favorite target, Peter Tsokanis, BC '52, who inspired Coach Tansey's immortal "Brockton" play.

1953

1971

WENTWORTH HALL

The Beatty Era, 1953-1971

Just as historians record eras in terms of B.C. and A.D., so does the chronicle of Wentworth's history pivot on a defining midstream moment: the 1953 arrival of President H. Russell Beatty.

Through dedication, foresight, and force of will, Russ Beatty reinvented Wentworth Institute. Wentworth before Beatty was an accomplished school for sure, but not one that caused other institutions to take much notice. Beatty's influence turned the Institute into a pioneer and trend-setter in technology education.

President Beatty brought radical change to Wentworth. In 1953, the trustees had felt mostly content with the state of the Institute. The newcomer Beatty held a different view. In effect, he inspected the institution he was inheriting and gave it a respectable C+. Whereas Dobbs' Wentworth maintained the status quo, Beatty wanted his Wentworth to shake off its inertia and reach for something higher.

The Wentworth that Beatty signed on with was essentially a high-octane trade school. The president immediately set about creating another species altogether, a more highly evolved breed of technical school.

Top left: Dr. H. Russell Beatty, principal for two weeks, president for 18 years.

Left: The Institute's first dormitory, Wentworth Hall. Trustees bought the Evans Way property from Gordon College in 1955.

Below: President Beatty acts as official greeter at the start of the 1960 school year.

A Matter of Degrees

President Beatty and his family welcome trustee John Volpe and his wife to Wentworth Institute's 50th birthday party in September 1954. The president's wife, Alice, is at his side; their son, Robert, is at far right.

Priority number one for Beatty was elevating the Institute to the status of a junior college. For decades, Wentworth occupied a sort of higher education purgatory: more than a high school, less than a college. The education establishment nationwide refused to adopt a protocol for conferring degrees to pupils who underwent the technical education offered by schools like Wentworth. A certain class-based snobbery underscored this refusal, consisting of Ivy League-educated men who perceived Wentworth's academic profile as glorified vocational-technical training. The idea that such a track merited degree consideration was heretical to these men.*

By the early 1950s, it fell upon a few men of missionary zeal to lobby for advanced standing for technical schools. Russ Beatty was one of these men. Like Arthur Williston, he had forged his educational philosophy at Pratt Institute in Brooklyn, N.Y., where he taught for 16 years and was dean of the College of Engineering. Pratt had offered bachelor's degrees since 1938. This shaped Beatty's thinking when he jumped to Wentworth in 1953. A month after arriving, he began right away to educate his bosses, the trustees, that Wentworth should try to amend its charter, granting the Institute the right to offer associate's degrees. Externally, he led the effort to convince the Massachusetts Collegiate Authority to get on board with the proposal. A sort of two-step resulted: Beatty, convinced of his rightness, offered Wentworth Institute as a test case to demonstrate the merits of technical schools. The MCA, swayed by his eager advocacy, eventually complied.

In the end, both sides were pleased with the results.

In 1956, Wentworth amended its charter. A year later, the Institute awarded its first associate in engineering degrees to 294 men who received their diplomas during commencement ceremonies at Symphony Hall. (In addition, the next year, 1958, saw 58 graduates from the classes of 1952-1956 complete supplementary courses to upgrade their certificates to associate's degrees. One of these men was future board chairman, Robert Boyden, MC&TD '52.) Wentworth Institute had entered a new era.

---

*This schism dated back to the 19th century. Robert McMath's book, *Engineering the New South*, identifies the origins: "Two contrasting approaches to the education of mechanical engineers [in the mid-to-late 19th century] reflected a conflict between two cultures—the shop culture and the school culture. The cultural conflict resulted in the creation of two major types of mechanical engineering colleges. One type, designed by the leaders of the school culture, included such colleges as the Stevens Institute of Technology and the Massachusetts Institute of Technology. Engineering programs in these schools stressed higher mathematics, theoretical science, and original research. An alternative college, preferred by proponents of the shop culture, included the Worcester Free Institute and the Rose Polytechnic Institute. These programs placed greater stress on practical shop work and produced graduates who could work as machinists or as shop foremen, but who were not well prepared for engineering analysis or original research.

"One leading proponent stressed the distinction between a technical institute such as Stevens and a 'trade school' such as Worcester. He suggested that the graduates of the technical school would be members of a profession that would be served by the trade school graduates. He proposed that the mechanical engineer should be educated as a 'designer of construction, not a constructor.' One is best suited for intellectual pursuits, the other is endowed with 'constructive faculties.'"

It's tempting to look back now and assume that this progress was preordained. It was not, however. Other schools of Wentworth's type—Franklin Institute in Boston, for one—ventured more tentatively, and less successfully, through these stages of growth. Both Wentworth and Franklin received authorization to grant associate's degrees in the mid-1950s. By 1970, Franklin offered six degree programs; Wentworth, on the other hand, boasted 19 thriving degree programs. And Franklin never blossomed into a baccalaureate-level institution, as Wentworth did. How had Wentworth found the magic touch with its degree programs? The credit belonged to President Beatty's bold, even stubborn, stewardship of the cause.

1957-58, WENTWORTH BEGAN OFFERING EVENING DEGREE PROGRAMS. THE FIRST CLASS CONSISTED OF 136 STUDENTS.

Below: Russ Beatty boasted strong academic credentials. While at Pratt Institute, he co-authored the textbook, *Principles of Industrial Management*.

Below right: For decades, a minimalist approach to landscaping dominated at Wentworth.

"Engineering technology education must be *sold*," wrote Beatty. "You can build the best mousetrap in the world, but the world will not beat a path to your door unless you convince people that you indeed have the best mousetrap. The same is true of educational endeavors. We know that we are doing a quality job in this educational field, but we have to convince the young people of this country that this is so. We also have to sell them on the worthwhileness of a career in engineering technology, not only because it is remunerative, but also because it is important work to do."

The American Society for Engineering Education recognized this pioneering work when it presented Beatty with the James H. McGraw Award in 1961. The ASEE cited his "indefatigable crusading for technical institute education, and for his developmental work in promoting a better understanding of, and more effective role for, the technician in our industrial society."

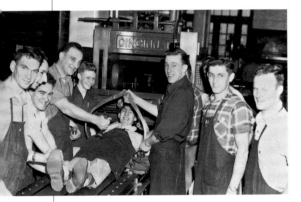

Above: Machine Work students in 1953 enjoy their salad days. The Wentworth men are committing approximately 17 safety violations in the above photo—luckily for them, the Occupational Safety & Health Administration was still 18 years from being founded.

Top: Hank Hesse, MW '53, in the machine shop.

The Ascent of Engineering Technology

Russ Beatty didn't invent engineering technology. But it's easy to assume he did. Engineering technicians, however, had been around long before Wentworth was founded. They just didn't have that title. Or much respect. Still, the engineering technician had become a vital cog in American industry by the 1950s.

As U.S. Secretary of Commerce Sinclair Weeks Sr. noted in a 1957 address, "There is a growing need for supporting workers—draftsmen, laboratory assistants, and other technicians—without whom the efficiency and the progress of the engineer would be critically curtailed or utterly lost. For every professional researcher, the educational branches of our economy must provide two supporting workers."

Beatty was a tireless ambassador of engineering technology, constantly beating the drum to high schools, professional societies, newspapers, and whoever else would listen. Here's how he described the field to a gathering of high school guidance counselors in 1957: "The engineering technician is the liaison man between the engineer and the craftsman; the chief petty officer of industry, if you please. He interprets the engineer's designs to the craftsman so that the product can be built economically. He supervises the craftsman in the construction of buildings, machines, electronic devices, rockets, aircraft, and the like. He works with the engineer in the research laboratory on the construction of experimental models of new devices."

Engineering technology programs, noted Beatty, were "more practical and intensive than those given in engineering colleges, and more advanced in character than those given in trade schools. The education consists of a balanced arrangement of classroom, laboratory, drafting room, and shop work. The student learns by doing as well as by studying and listening so that he can apply his knowledge to practical production and construction problems."

But engineering technology suffered a problem of perception. Engineering technicians were in-betweeners, professionally speaking. And technical institutes like Wentworth, Beatty complained in 1956, had been misunderstood and underappreciated for more than 50 years. The president called this a "status barrier."

A huge boost over this status barrier was achieved in 1956 when Wentworth Institute successfully petitioned for the right to change its charter to grant associate in engineering degrees. (In 1958, the Institute began awarding associate in applied science degrees as well.) Another boost came in 1967 when, after years of fierce campaigning by Beatty, Wentworth Institute became the first two-year technical school to be accredited by the New England Association of Schools and Colleges.

As engineering technology gained status in academia, its standing in industry followed suit. During the '60s and '70s, engineering technicians attained greater prestige in the workplace, and enjoyed greater earning power as well. Between 1967 and 1976, engineering technician jobs increased by 76 percent and salaries rose by 60 percent.

From the day he arrived on campus, President Beatty emphasized the importance of a high-quality library.

Above: Initially, the library was housed on the narrow mezzanine level of Watson Hall.

Right: Its next location was the second floor of the Main Building.

Above right: When Beatty Hall opened in 1967, Wentworth's Physical Plant employees hatched an ingenious system to move the books into the new library. Instead of lugging books up and down four flights of stairs, they hung a wire between the Main Building and Beatty Hall, and winched the texts across the quad.

PIONEERING PROGRAMS

Russ Beatty relished being ahead of the curve when it came to developing academic initiatives at Wentworth. He was a striver. His stewardship of the nuclear engineering technology program offers an example.

In 1958, not a school in the world was educating nuclear engineering technicians. Not only was it a nascent field, but also one governed by secrecy. Since World War II, the federal government had monopolized the training of technicians in its laboratories at Oak Ridge and Argonne. But Wentworth Institute had an inside track on breaking the monopoly. The chairman of its board, Sinclair Weeks Sr., happened to be serving in Washington, D.C., as President Eisenhower's Secretary of Commerce. Weeks tipped off Beatty to the untapped opportunity, and Wentworth's president quickly formed a committee to explore the possibility of developing such an academic program. After four years, a quarter of a million dollars (including three grants from the Atomic Energy Commission), and a new 7,300-square-foot building (Willson Hall), Wentworth unveiled the nation's first nuclear engineering technology program in 1962.

Below: The nuclear engineering technology program debuted in 1962.

Below right: Strength of materials lab, 1965.

Having kept close vigil on Wentworth's pioneering work, dozens of schools followed suit with programs geared to training nuclear technicians. Hundreds of students graduated from the program at Wentworth between 1963 and 1979, when the Three Mile Island disaster finally decimated whatever appeal nuclear energy once held for 18-year-olds.

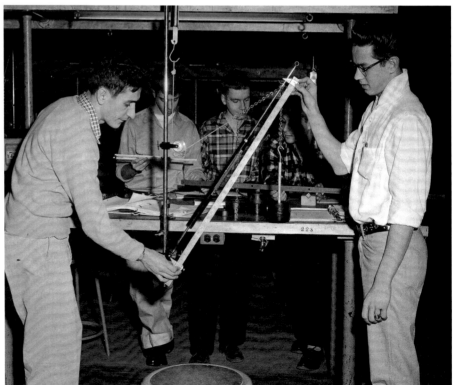

Aeronautical technology was one of several majors pioneered by Wentworth during the '50s and '60s.

Heavy materials lab, 1960. The student at right is taking serious liberties with the Wentworth dress code; his T-shirt attire was definitely not Beatty-approved.

In addition to nuclear engineering technology, President Beatty pioneered several other academic programs. Wentworth's civil and highway engineering program, which debuted in 1958, was the first in the nation. Materials engineering technology and aeronautical and space engineering technology were two other first-of-their-kind majors.

Russ Beatty was not a boastful man, but even he couldn't resist when the topic touched on the Institute's sudden primacy in its specialized niche of higher education: "During my years here," he wrote, "the educational standards of the Institute have been raised to the point where its leadership position in engineering technology education is recognized nationally and internationally."

Above: President Beatty was not a fan of the "Wentworth Institute Alma Mater" that had been in place since the early '20s. It was a little too cute for his liking. ("Twas many years ago, dear boys, a man of high repute, endowed our Alma Mater, the Wentworth Institute....") So, in 1956, Beatty staged a songwriting contest in which he invited faculty, staff, and students to submit entries for a new school song. The winning lyricist was Ashlyn Huyck, a mathematics instructor. Putting music to Huyck's words was Edward Whittredge, choir director of the Wollaston Congregational Church and a close friend of the Beattys. Their Alma Mater remains the school song to this day.

Right: Instructor John Bruce supervises mechanical design students as they fashion a coupling, 1960.

WE WORK HARDER

Wentworth students have always worked hard. Since the first year of classes in 1911-12, Wentworth operated on much the same lines as the industries that scooped up its graduates. Forty-hour weeks were the standard unit of measurement for Wentworth students. You showed up at eight in the morning. You took a half-hour for lunch. You headed back to the classroom or the lab until four in the afternoon. The only thing missing was a punch clock.

Paul Berenson, NET '65, remembers the tough regimen: "It was actually a grind. I felt more like I was going to work than to college. I would leave the house at 7:00 for an 8:00 class, work straight through until 4:00, then go to an after-school job. I usually fell asleep at night with my face in a book."

Still, during the first half of the 20th century, Wentworth wasn't all that unique—plenty of colleges worked their students hard. Not until the 1960s did a gap arise between how hard (or how long) Wentworth students worked and how hard (or not) students at most other colleges worked. During the last 40 years, as well-pedigreed colleges have ushered in course schedules calling for 24-hour weeks and, later, 16-hour and even 12-hour weeks, Wentworth has relented very little on its grueling standard. Over the last decade or two, the Institute has "relaxed" to about a 30-hour average week. But that's still twice as demanding a schedule as that endured by most of Boston's other 247,000 college students. This disparity has always been a badge of honor for Wentworth students. And probably always will be.

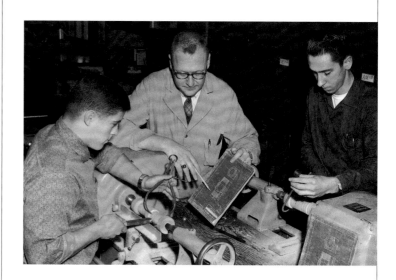

Basic industries have
always played a key role
in Wentworth's curriculum.

Clockwise from top left:
Welding class, 1965.
Masonry project, 1970.
Students pour a mold in
the foundry under the
watchful eye of instructor
Robert Edwards, 1970.

A Building Bonanza

As their ambitions for Wentworth grew, President Beatty and the trustees needed to expand the physical plant to contain them. Under his leadership, the Boston campus tripled in size. During his 18-year tenure, he greenlighted the construction of five new buildings (comprising 222,000 square feet) and acquired four more (totaling 216,000 square feet). Much of this square footage was dedicated to living space—Wentworth purchased a dormitory (today known as Tudbury Hall) from Gordon College in 1955, and a decade later bought a pair of apartment buildings (today known as Edwards/Rodgers Hall) next to the firehouse on Huntington Avenue, and another residence hall on the corner of Evans Way and the Fenway (today known as Evans Way). As demand grew, the Institute broke ground on its first brand-new dormitory, Baker Hall, in 1971. This investment in residential property offers another example of President Beatty being ahead of his time. When he arrived at Wentworth in 1953, 19 out of 20 students commuted to campus. He grasped, before anyone else did, the far-reaching benefits of changing that ratio.

An aerial view of campus, 1960. The baseball diamond on the quad survived another six years, until the Institute broke ground on its general purpose building, Beatty Hall.

Right: Beatty Hall, circa 1988. Its brutalist style reflected a prevailing architectural trend of the late '60s. The facility has not aged gracefully, however. Thirty-seven years after its arrival, Beatty Hall has few admirers on campus.

Below: The first few concrete forms of Beatty Hall, 1967.

Boston wasn't the only site of campus growth. In 1956, the Institute purchased 155 undeveloped acres in Plainville, Massachusetts, for use as instruction grounds for civil and construction engineering technology students.

Such dramatic campus growth exacted a high fee. And trustees were adamant that tuition not be increased at a rate burdensome to applicants. This meant that fund raising suddenly became a priority for the president. The task did not come naturally to Beatty. Yet, he tackled the job with vigor and without complaint. Development Director Charlie Pheeney recalls, "If I were holding an alumni meeting, no matter where it was or how far away, Dr. Beatty would always get in his car to go out and meet the people. That's just the sort of man he was. He inspired loyalty."

He and Pheeney succeeded in raising enough money to support Wentworth's growing needs. (Day students had increased fourfold, from 500 to 2,000, between 1954 and 1964.) In the mid-1960s, the Institute initiated a capital campaign. The school's $3-million goal focused on three major bricks-and-mortar projects: a recreation center, a dormitory, and a general purpose building consisting of a library, cafeteria, and classrooms.

The campaign worked as planned. Wentworth opened its general purpose building in 1967 under the name of Beatty Hall (the trustees insisted that no other name be considered). Everything about it, including its contemporary architecture, announced an entirely new era at Wentworth. The Nelson Recreation Center arrived in 1969, and the Baker Hall dormitory opened in 1971.

20. Alice Beatty

The First Lady

Although Russ Beatty ran Wentworth for two decades, many students from that era remember his wife more vividly. Mrs. Beatty was not a

demure, retiring first lady, content merely to stand at her husband's elbow during campus receptions. Rather, she was a force to reckon with, as committed to the Institute's operation as any administrator. One of her passions was the decor of campus buildings; the 1956 renovation of the administrative office, for instance, bore her mark—she chose the layout, office equipment, and color scheme. Later, she championed the interior design scheme that ultimately enlivened the 30,000-square-foot library in the building that bore her husband's name. But in student circles, her legendary status sprang primarily from her full-blooded artistic direction of annual events such as academic convocations and spring concerts. "The first thing we'd do is stand up and sing all four verses of the Wentworth Alma Mater," recalls Charlie Cimino, AET '68, AE '74. "We'd always be led by Mrs. Beatty, who had a bright soprano voice but wasn't always on key." Only two things were more piercing than Mrs. Beatty's singing voice: her devotion to her husband and her interest in the well-being of Wentworth students. Students from far-flung addresses fondly remember her as a gracious hostess during holiday dinners at the Beatty home in Quincy, Mass. George Chryssis, EET '69, who had come to Wentworth from Greece, recalls Thanksgiving 1968: "Dr. and Mrs. Beatty picked up the foreign students at Wentworth in two cars and drove us to their house. We had a very nice dinner with all the trimmings. Mrs. Beatty sat at the piano and sang some songs. They were both very cordial; it was a lovely day."

21. H. Russell Beatty

The Visionary

The second half of Wentworth's first century began, literally and figuratively, with H. Russell Beatty. He ended the era of principals and initiated the run of presidents. (He was hired as principal, but a couple of weeks into the job, he requested a title upgrade from the trustees. They assented.) No other principal or president ever placed a stronger stamp on the school. For 18 years, from 1953 to 1971, he was the alpha and omega of all things Wentworth. History has shown his strategic vision to be very keen. A month into his tenure, for instance, he wrote to the trustees, "The trend is definitely toward the use of the associate's degree by technical institutes, and we should be a leader in this movement rather than one of the last to come in." Two years later, the Institute amended its charter to offer associate's degrees. He showed the same shrewd foresight in many other areas. He vigilantly maintained an up-to-date curriculum. He inherited 10 academic programs in 1953; by 1969, there were 18. Only two of the original 10 programs had survived in any recognizable form. He more than doubled the campus, erecting five

new buildings and purchasing four more. He built the school's first legitimate library and gymnasium and created a residential campus from scratch. And in 1970, much as he had done 17 years earlier, Beatty launched Wentworth College of Technology, a baccalaureate-level institution. Despite all this, many alumni remember him not for his accomplishments, but for his despotic ways: they regard him as a man who ruled the school with a wise head, but an iron hand and a hard heart.

22. Richard Newton, MC&TD '42

The Cold Warrior

No person yet, of course, has been tagged with the ignominious distinction of having started World War III. But Wentworth graduate Richard Newton came as close as anyone to earning the cursed label. Major Newton knew real war. During World War II, he ran nearly 100 bomber raids from the Marshall Islands, targeting enemy airfields and supply sites. Later, he learned that undeclared wars were more treacherous. In the early '50s, Newton began a 27-year career with the CIA. In 1960, he was the executive officer and senior CIA operative with the U-2 Air Force

detachment when Russia shot down the spy plane piloted by his good friend, Francis Gary Powers. As the superpowers rattled their sabers, Newton waited anxiously to learn his own fate. "I thought I was going to lose my mind," he said. "Fortunately, President Eisenhower looked at me and said, 'I don't want to stick it to this little middle-level guy. He's no general, so I'm not going to shaft him.' So, he took the blame. Thank God for him." Even in his retirement, Newton continues to live dangerously. Now in his 80s, he is the oldest registered hang glider pilot in the United States.

23. Charles Pheeney, EC '48

The Fund Raiser

Today, Wentworth Institute of Technology raises more than two million dollars each year to support its mission. Every dollar that comes in builds on a foundation laid by Charlie Pheeney. In 1946, after having served 34 months in the Pacific Theater during World War II, where he rose to the rank of technical sergeant, Pheeney returned stateside and enrolled in Wentworth's electrical construction program with the assistance of the GI Bill. Unfortunately, he nearly flunked out of Wentworth during his first semester due to a miscalculation in a series and parallel circuit exam. Principal Frederick Dobbs, however, let him retake the exam, which he passed easily. In hindsight, it was a $16 million decision by Mr. Dobbs. That's how much money Charlie Pheeney went on to raise for his alma mater. In 1956, President

H. Russell Beatty hired the graduate to be the Institute's alumni secretary. Pheeney served in that role until 1963, when a $3,000,000 fund raising campaign spurred Beatty to make him the school's first-ever director of development. Pheeney flourished in that role for the next 22 years, shepherding the Institute through two major capital campaigns. He raised money not through slick salesmanship, but rather a prevailing sense of decency and commitment to the Institute. A 1985 Alumni News article demystified Pheeney's knack for fund raising: "Many years ago he addressed a group of alumni and related the needs of Wentworth. After the meeting, a chap, modestly garbed, came up to Charlie and said that as a result of the talk he was going to divide his estate of about $50,000 between Wentworth and his wife's charity. 'He had no visible signs of affluence,' said Pheeney. 'It shows that being sensitive to people's wishes and needs pays off.'"

24. Joseph Tansey
The Coach

Most everyone today agrees that a full-bodied collegiate experience contributes mightily to the mission of Wentworth; that students' development outside the classroom is as fundamental as their formal education. More than any other individual, Joe Tansey nurtured this philosophy at Wentworth. He was a Norwich University graduate who arrived at

Wentworth in 1933 to teach English and public speaking ("Get to the crux of things!" he often exhorted in the classroom.) Each day at 4 p.m., Tansey set aside the books and strapped a whistle around his neck. Coach Tansey was nothing if not versatile. In the fall, he coached football; in the winter, basketball; and in the spring, baseball. More than 1,000 Wentworth athletes enjoyed his tutelage. During World War II, Captain Tansey served for three years in the Pacific Theater as an intelligence officer for an Air Force bomb group. The war turned Tansey's hair completely gray. Even had it not, the 1953 arrival of Russ Beatty probably would have done the trick. Student affairs were hardly Beatty's strong point. But, to his credit, he knew to whom to entrust the job. In 1955, he appointed Tansey as the Institute's first dean of students. He served in that role until his retirement in 1968. "He would do anything to help a student," recalls his daughter, Gail Tansey Catanzaro. "Sometimes he'd even invite students to stay at our house if they were having trouble finding a place to live near campus. They'd commute to school together from Winchester." In 1968, the Institute dedicated its gymnasium in Tansey's name, a fitting tribute to the man known as the "Father of Wentworth Athletics." And in 2001, Wentworth got to the crux of things by inducting Joe Tansey posthumously into the inaugural class of its Athletics Hall of Fame.

25. H. Prescott Tucker Jr., EI&M '37
The Caretaker

H. Prescott Tucker was vintage Wentworth, a great example of the fashion of man who tended to graduate from the Institute: hard working,

efficient, and humble. "Tuck" earned a certificate in electrical installation and maintenance in 1937, and returned six years later to his alma mater, where he worked for the next 33 years. He taught electric wiring

in the evening school and instructed Navy machinist's mates during World War II. He also wired the nosecones of V-2 rockets when Wentworth first began working on Air Force Contracts in the late 1940s. But he made his greatest impact on Wentworth as superintendent of building and grounds. "Tuck was a campus institution," wrote Professor George Freimarck. "With a mere handful of assistants it seemed he practically ran the place physically—quietly, smoothly, no fuss, no red tape. If anything of a maintenance nature needed doing, a phone call to Tuck would get it done, and usually within the day." He was a striking man with a handsome face that looked like it was carved out of granite, silver hair set off by shaggy black eyebrows, startling blue eyes, and his trademark bow tie. In addition, he was a cheerful colleague despite suffering from crippling arthritis in later years. Harry Bertschy, English department head, recalls, "Once I pleaded with Tuck to be a little easier on himself and not be so generous in helping others. His answer revealed his character. 'Harry,' he said, 'The good Lord seems to give it to those who can take it.'"

26. John Volpe, AC '30
The Governor

Wentworth's most famous alumnus was also one of its most loyal. A 1930 architectural construction graduate, John Volpe visited his alma mater

hundreds of times over the years, including a 14-year stint as trustee. All while building incredibly successful careers in both the private and public sectors—an unprecedented track record for a Wentworth alumnus. Son of an Italian immigrant, Volpe grew up in Malden, Mass. Forced to abandon his plan to attend Massachusetts Institute of Technology when his father's plastering business hit hard times, Volpe enrolled instead at Wentworth. After graduating, he overcame Depression-era obstacles and started a construction company that in two decades time became one of the nation's largest. In the 1950s, Volpe entered public service and in 1956 was named the first federal highway administrator by President Dwight D. Eisenhower. He played a central role in the development of the nation's Interstate Highway System. After he returned home in 1960, voters elected Volpe to a two-year term as Republican governor of Massachusetts. He won again in 1964 as well as 1966, but left midway through his third term to accept the Secretary of Transportation Cabinet position in the Nixon administration. Two of his pet projects were the federalization of passenger rail service

and a push—25 years ahead of its time—to install safety air bags in automobiles. From 1972 to 1976, Volpe served as ambassador to Italy. In 1980, he received the first honorary doctorate ever awarded by Wentworth Institute of Technology. Although it was the 32nd honorary degree he received in his lifetime, he noted that it meant more to him than any other because it had come from "this great institution...my alma mater."

27, 28. Sinclair Weeks Sr. and Sinclair Weeks Jr.
The Trustees

No name entwines itself more intrinsically into the scroll of Wentworth history than Weeks. For a combined 96 years and counting (Sinclair

Weeks Sr. for 43 years and Sinclair Weeks Jr. in his 53rd year), the father and son have been mainstays on Wentworth's board of trustees. The elder Sinclair Weeks joined the board in 1928. In 1930, he was elected mayor of Newton, Mass. He went on to even greater glory—appointed to the U.S. Senate in 1944, and named Secretary of Commerce by President Dwight D. Eisenhower in 1953. That year, he also ascended to the chairmanship of Wentworth's board of trustees. He served in this role for a record 19 years, a tenure that paralleled the presidency of H. Russell Beatty. He gave Beatty considerable autonomy in directing the Institute's course, a wise decision. Of all the good things Sinclair Weeks Sr. did for Wentworth, though, perhaps the greatest occurred when he introduced his son to the Institute's service. The board elected Sinclair Weeks Jr., chairman of the Reed and Barton Corporation in Taunton, Mass., as a Wentworth trustee in 1951. Fifty-three years later, he continues to serve on the board. He held the chair from 1976 to 1981. But of the hundreds of important decisions for which he offered counsel during his 53 years on the board, he made his biggest splash one year into his tenure. In 1952, the board appointed Weeks as head of the search committee to replace Principal Frederick Dobbs. His father-in-law suggested he contact Henry Heald, president of Armour Institute of Technology in Chicago, and later president of the Ford Foundation. Dr. Heald put his full support behind an up-and-comer at Pratt Institute named Russ Beatty. The next day, Weeks contacted Beatty and the rest is Wentworth history.

A Brief Glimpse of Why It Costs So Much to Administer an Engineering Technology Academic Program

The civil and highway engineering program began with 48 students in September 1957. The Institute built a satellite campus on a 155-acre tract in Plainville, Mass., constructed a laboratory building and other ancillary structures, and added three instructors to the teaching staff. And that only accounted for half the battle. As President Beatty described in the 1957-58 Annual Report, "In the fall, the laboratory equipment consisted only of a station wagon, 10 surveying instruments, and a variety of hand tools including axes, picks, shovels, bush cutters, and the like." So, how did the Institute manage to equip the program in the matter of just a few months? Money helped, of course, but Wentworth also got a little help from a lot of friends:

THE FOLLOWING ITEMS WERE DONATED:

BAYER & MINGOLLA CONSTRUCTION CO.
1/2-ton pickup truck, jack hammer, paving breaker drill steel, air hose, concrete pipe, small tools

BLACKHAWK MANUFACTURING CO.
Ram, gauges, valves, and automatic pump

CHISHOLM-MOORE HOIST DIVISION
1-ton Cyclone Model M chain hoist

CARL HEINRICH CO.
Kern 9K1-C level with tripod

INGERSOLL-RAND CO.
125 cfm compressor and tools

KEUFFEL & ESSER CO.
1 planimeter #4236, two 5137 transits, one 5003 level, 3 tripods 5191-8

LITTLEFORD BROTHERS INC.
Model 700 Trail-O-Patcher Bituminous Mixer, True-Lay Paver Spreader

LOMBARD GOVERNOR CORP.
Model 44 20" chain saw

B.L. MAKEPEACE INC.
Assorted surveying & drawing materials

MALL TOOL CO.—DIV. OF REMINGTON ARMS
Remington Golden Logmaster 24" chain saw

MARLOW PUMP DIV. OF BELL & GOSSETT CO.
Marlow Model 3B7 contractors pump, 3" contractors diaphragm pump

MASTER VIBRATOR CO.
Concrete vibrator

PERINI CORP.
Koehring Model 304 3/4 yd. backhoe

ROWCO CO.
Brush King Cutter

SASGEN DERRICK CO.
No. 110 winch, B-5-T winch

TEMPLETON, KENLY, & CO.
6 trench braces & hydraulic jack with 100-ton ram

JOHN A. VOLPE CONSTRUCTION CO.
Gasoline generator set, hardware, nails, lumber, reinforcement steel

GALION IRON WORKS & MFG. CO.
5/8-ton tandem roller

PERKINS MACHINERY CO.
Caterpillar D4 bulldozer

KOEHRING DIV. OF KOEHRING CO.
Model 304 shovel attachment

BOSTON SAND & GRAVEL CO.
Transit cement mixer

COLEMAN BROTHERS
Dump truck

NATIONAL CRUSHED STONE ASSOCIATION
Hummer Electric Screen

THE FOLLOWING ITEMS WERE PURCHASED:

B. L. MAKEPEACE INC.
Planimeter

NERNEY MOTOR SALES
1957 Ford Ranch Wagon

SEABOARD SUPPLY
Legal-size steel file cabinet

KEUFFEL & ESSER CO.
Leveling rods, tripods, curves, transits

SEARS & ROEBUCK
10" power saw

CENTRAL SCIENTIFIC
Sieves

R.G. MEARN CO.
Skil drill, Skil saw

DEWITT'S GARAGE
1957 Chevrolet truck

President Beatty concluded this daunting list with a sobering postscript: "We shall need to acquire another $75,000 worth of road building machinery, and the laboratory will need to have $200,000 worth of equipment to bring it up to the standards that prevail in our other laboratories."

LORD OF DISCIPLINE

Progressive as he was in plotting the big picture for Wentworth, Dr. Beatty's leadership was remarkably throwback in other areas. Twenty years ahead of his time in some ways, twenty years behind it in others.

Life at Wentworth may have been heavily routinized under President Beatty. But it was never dull.

The Beatty years were infamous for the concept that students called "forced fun." Beatty, who put great stock in the cliché that "an idle mind is the devil's workshop," hijacked perhaps the only free hour of the students' busy academic week, and instituted a policy of mandatory enrichment. Whether that enrichment took the form of a glee club performance or a calisthenics regimen was ultimately irrelevant. The important detail for students to remember? Participation was not voluntary. In order to receive the necessary credit, while at the same time maintaining a shred of self-determination, many Beatty-era students adopted a forced fun survival strategy—they formed their own clubs: the whist club, the model railroad club (with an impressive track on the roof level of Williston Hall), and the folk singing club, to name just a few.

Folk singers notwithstanding, Beatty's Wentworth was a well-groomed, buttoned-up, tightly regulated bastion of order. George Chryssis, EET '69, jokes today, "It wasn't until after I entered Wentworth that I realized it was a military academy."

From the time he began his presidency in 1953 through the turbulent decades of the '60s and early '70s, Beatty's adherence to strict discipline became the stuff of legend.

Below: Forced fun? On the contrary, these members of the 1965 model railroad club appear to genuinely enjoy their free-time enterprise.

Below right: Members of the 1962 dance band club also seem reasonably enthusiastic.

Extracurricular activities during the 1960s ran the gamut from incendiary to positively angelic.

This page, clockwise from top, all from 1966: The pistol club; wrought iron club; and leather-craft club.

Opposite page, top left: The 1962 rifle team.

Top right: The 1960 glee club, an organization whose advisor and muse was the president's wife, Mrs. Alice Beatty.

Below: Perhaps Dr. Beatty was inspired to initiate his push for "extracurricular enrichment" after witnessing lackadaisical student behavior such as this 1956 smoking break on the front steps of the Main Building.

Of All the Windows to Break...

Bob Lazarus, PET '61, a power-hitting rightfielder on the baseball team, was the only student in Wentworth history nearly kicked out of school for hitting a home run.

One afternoon, during a game on Wentworth's home field, the lefty slugger belted the longest home run seen on Huntington Avenue since the Red Sox left the Ball Grounds in 1912. It soared far over the center fielder's head and crashed through a first-story window in the back of the Main Building. Home-crowd cheers immediately turned to sickening silence. Lazarus circled the bases with a sinking feeling in his gut. Wentworth teammates and fans stared in horror at the home run's resting place. Everyone knew that the window Lazarus had just shattered belonged to the office of President Beatty. And if a sideburn one inch too long could get you thrown out of class, imagine what breaking Beatty's window would get you! Everyone held their breath as Mr. Beatty strode to the window, picked up the baseball, examined it with scientific curiosity, and then proceeded to...smile. Athletes and spectators let loose a huge collective sigh of relief, Bob Lazarus' loudest of all.

Bob Lazarus shows the hitting form that nearly ended his Wentworth career.

Hairy Days

During Russ Beatty's last two years as president of Wentworth Institute, hair was the hottest of numerous hot-button topics on campus. In 1970, a group of fed-up students formed the provocatively-named protest group, S.M.U.T. (Student Movement to Undermine Tyranny). In one of their pamphlets, they fired this shot across the administration's bow:

"When a student attends his first Wentworth convocation in the fall of his first year, he is told by Dr. Beatty that he now has the good fortune to be enrolled in the finest two-year technical school in this country. The Wentworth graduate will possess technical knowledge and skill far surpassing that of any other technical institute's graduates, save for MIT and (perhaps) the Caltech men.

"Employers throughout the nation, says Dr. Beatty, are aware of our valuable skills, and once we have graduated from Wentworth we need never again, it seems, worry about being left jobless or even underpaid.

"SO WHY THEN if our graduates are held in such regard for their abilities, is the administration of Wentworth afraid that the student will be passed by if his HAIR HAPPENS TO TOUCH HIS COLLAR?"

Later, the SMUTsters voiced their objections more poetically:

Some rules are for our safety,
"Sideburns are worn short," they said.
"They get caught easily in drafting pencils,
"And then you're good as dead."

"Long hair and beards are not allowed,
They make you look like a slob
Like those freaks at Yale and Harvard
You'll never get a job."

They tell me exactly what I must do
Each second of the day
I'm not allowed to think for myself,
"It's much better for me that way."

Dissent rocks the Wentworth campus, 1970. Clearly, the moustached students were not seasoned protestors; their sign, "Revise Dress Code" signaled a willingness to compromise on the opening gambit, a classic negotiating miscue.

Take the matter of hair. Early on, Beatty established a dress code for students at the Institute, which went so far as to set requirements for hair length, sideburn length, and facial hair dos and don'ts. Charlie Cimino, AET '68, AE '74, who is now an architecture professor at Wentworth, remembers it with a laugh: "One of my classmates was in charge of monitoring hair length. Every so often he'd tell me my sideburns were too long—they weren't supposed to go below the middle of your ear." [*See "Hairy Days" at left.*]

A rule was a rule in Dr. Beatty's mind, and he never wavered from that during his presidency, no matter how silly the battleground. This became clear in 1970, when the hair issue reached the courts. It happened when a Wentworth student committed a blasphemous act: he grew a beard. As these were expressly forbidden, President Beatty threw the rebel out of class. (The 1970 Student Handbook dedicated two full pages to *Deportment*: "Wentworth Institute has the right and the obligation to intervene when new fads in hair styling, clothing, and the general appearance of students interfere with learning and are disruptive of classroom morale.") Incredibly, the dispute ultimately traveled to the federal district court, which ended up ruling in the school's favor. Clean-shavedness at Wentworth lived to see another day.

Starting in the late 1960s, of course, college students nationwide began to rebel against long-held codes of appearance, attitude, and behavior. Catalyzed in large part by the Vietnam War, revolt became almost the norm at campuses throughout the country. It was a trying time for Dr. Beatty the disciplinarian. But he kept up the good fight, varying his approach from hands off to hands on.

In 1970, a group of Wentworth students finally saw fit to stage a protest on campus. They marched in front of Wentworth Hall, shouting and holding signs that objected to the dress code and other affronts. Visitors to Beatty's office, which stood 50 feet away from the protest, observed that he simply ignored the tumult, acting as if all the screaming outside just wasn't happening. Later, in his message for the class yearbook, Beatty gave the "revolt" a distinctly conformist spin: "As a class, you have contributed to the dialogue among students, faculty, and administration that has now become part of the higher education scene. You have made your desire for changes known without bringing discredit to your alma mater and to yourself. You will benefit from your decision to govern your actions in this way."

Charlie Cimino recalls a more hands-on response to some rule bending that occurred in 1968: "Wentworth had always held very formal dances. That year, though, we organized a college mixer that would have singles. We invited girls from Simmons and Emmanuel and other schools. We even had a couple of rock bands, which was a first. Well, at about 9:30 that night, the hall was packed when President Beatty showed up at the dance. He was furious. Fuming. There were some people in attendance he felt shouldn't be there. So he just grabbed them by the collar and dragged them outside. Then he found our faculty

Edmund Turiello checks the work of drafting students, 1967.

advisor, tore into him in front of everyone, and finally said they'd meet about this matter the next morning." Problem solved.

This theme of Beatty as a bouncer pops up frequently in recollections of the president. One faculty member recalls his policy on tuition payments: "Colleges have all sorts of problems nowadays with students who are attending class but haven't fully paid their tuition. You didn't with Beatty. He'd personally come to the classroom and drag kids out who hadn't yet paid all their tuition."

While some students may have chafed under the discipline, the trustees thought Dr. Beatty walked on water. "Beatty was superb," says board member Sinclair Weeks Jr. "He was a great disciplinarian, which the school really needed then. There were a lot of problems at the time with younger people and the effects of the Vietnam War and drugs. Beatty made them toe the line. I know a number of students who were grateful to him for doing it."

Wentworth was a second family to H. Russell Beatty. "Wentworth was his life," says Charlie Pheeney, EC '48, "and anything you did to hurt it, he'd let you know." And like the father of a family, you couldn't sneak much past him. Some tell the story of Beatty glancing out his office window one afternoon and seeing a student strolling by. Not knowing the student specifically, but correctly divining that he belonged in class at that hour, Beatty sprang out of his chair, ran outside, grabbed the student by the arm and led him briskly to the appropriate classroom. Upon entering the room, Beatty sat the student down and then took time to chew out the instructor for allowing this tardiness to occur.

He cared deeply about the school and protected it diligently. "Whatever you do to injure Wentworth's reputation," he warned graduating students in 1968, "will lessen your own position in the community." He never missed an opportunity to bolster Wentworth's image. At a department meeting in 1967, he proclaimed that he knew places like Harvard and MIT were slipping, but Wentworth sure wasn't. Professor Bill Westland recalls a faculty meeting where the welding program, headed by Buono Rufo, started to come under fire. Beatty stood up and stopped the sniping in an instant. "Rufo and his boys are the finest welders you'll find anyplace," he boomed. And the welding instructors all beamed with pride.

Below: In 1966, Wentworth Institute purchased the Edwards/Rodgers residence hall on 572-574 Huntington Avenue. The apartments were built in 1924.

Below right: Dorm living, 1967.

So read the headline of an April 5, 1961, Wenitech student newspaper article about Wentworth's basketball team. The team's coach, Harry Bertschy, related a story about George Franklin, EEP '62, to illustrate that character is not measured in wins and losses:

"The Phillips Andover Academy game was scheduled for a Saturday afternoon. George works Saturdays until noon as a cab driver. On this particular Saturday, George rushed to Wentworth as soon as he had finished his work, only to find the school bus and the Wentworth team had already left for Andover. This did not deter him. He hitchhiked from Boston to Andover. Upon arriving there, he asked for directions to the academy but, in so doing, inadvertently referred to the academy as Exeter. On being told he was in the wrong town and headed for the wrong academy, he disappointedly returned to Boston.

"The fact that a player on a losing team, facing the possibility that he wouldn't get into the game, was willing to hitchhike twenty-odd miles certainly deserves commendation. It is this kind of attitude that breeds eventual success in life."

His care for the Institute ranged from the highest-level concerns to the most minute details of campus life. One day he noticed a truck in the parking lot that he felt was not being unloaded fast enough. So, he rolled up his suit sleeves, climbed aboard, and started hauling boxes off the truck. Another time, workers were laying carpet on the first floor of Wentworth Hall. Beatty wasn't pleased with the progress so he grabbed the hammer out of a worker's hand and started beating down the tacks himself.

"The guy worked ungodly hours," says Pheeney. "Most days he'd be in the office at five in the morning." Westland recalls Dr. Beatty and his wife leaving for a Caribbean cruise. "When they came back two weeks later, he was the same color as when he had left. As white as can be. He'd spent the whole vacation working in his cabin!"

Not once during his 18 years did Beatty cancel school due to bad weather. The president, however, did enjoy an unfair advantage on such occasions. He kept a small apartment across Huntington Avenue, on the third floor of the Collins Building. Anytime the forecast called for an overnight snowstorm, Beatty did not drive home to Quincy, but instead spent the night in his apartment. Early next morning, he'd wake up, trudge across the snow-covered street, shovel out the campus walkways, and then seat himself at the campus switchboard. Any optimists calling in to determine whether school was closed heard the answer in the president's gruff voice: "Of course there's school today! I expect to see you here on time."

His teaching philosophy revealed the same hard edge: "An educational program, to be effective," he wrote, "should require individuals to study some things which they do not enjoy….Life should not be made too easy for youth, lest they fail because of mental softness."

Sometimes this toughness could be taken too far. Joan Vater, wife of Clarence Vater, MDS '58, tells of her husband's experience with Dr. Beatty: "In 1957, after serving in the Navy and after the birth of our first son, Clarence's father died suddenly from a rare form of meningitis. It was just before Christmas and during exams. (Clarence had not missed a minute of classtime while I was in labor with our baby.) He went to President Beatty's office and requested permission to defer taking exams so that he could help in planning his father's funeral services. The president said no in a very negative manner."

Many alumni tell similar stories of slights suffered at the hands of H. Russell Beatty. But in the end, his reputation survives. Why? Charlie Pheeney sums it up well: "There were a lot of students who grumbled and growled about him and their time here. But then I'd see them down the road and they'd usually tell me, 'I'm so glad I was here when Dr. Beatty was. He made us do what we really needed to do.'"

Bachelor's Party

The Beatty era closed with a remarkable symmetry, the bookends being upgrades in institutional stature. On the front end of his Wentworth career, President Beatty had fast-tracked the jump to offering associate's degrees. Now, in the late 1960s, as his retirement loomed (he'd turn 65 in 1971), Beatty plotted the next advance for Wentworth.

In 1969, Beatty and the board of trustees applied to the Secretary of State of the Commonwealth of Massachusetts for the right to establish a new nonprofit educational corporation known as Wentworth College of Technology. The purpose of this new corporation was: "To furnish education in the mechanical arts, including engineering, with the right to grant bachelor of science, bachelor of engineering technology, and appropriate honorary degrees; to engage in research associated with such education, and to engage in other activities in the pursuit of such education and research."

IN APRIL 1970, THE ASSETS OF THE ARIOCH WENTWORTH ESTATE TURNED OVER TO WENTWORTH INSTITUTE FOLLOWING THE DEATH FOUR MONTHS EARLIER OF THE LAST LIFE INCOME BENEFICIARY. THE ASSETS WERE VALUED AT JUST UNDER $8.5 MILLION.

The application was successful. Beatty resigned as president of Wentworth Institute and the trustees named him president of Wentworth College of Technology. WCT welcomed its first class of students in September 1970. The College operated across the tracks on Huntington Avenue. For the first few years, it was headquartered in Tudbury Hall. Then in 1972, a new 13,000-square-foot building opened on 549 Huntington Avenue to house most of the College's operations.

Introducing an upper-level, baccalaureate-granting component at Wentworth was not a wildly radical idea. The Engineers' Council for Professional Development had started accrediting baccalaureate programs in engineering technology in 1966. Nevertheless, for Wentworth, the decision involved some risk.

The 1971 groundbreaking for Wentworth's first brand-new dormitory building, Baker Hall, on Huntington Avenue. From left, Charles Uppval, dean of students; Kenrick Baker, PM '13, longtime trustee and the building's namesake; Dr. Beatty; J.C. Bennett, vice president of the Austin Co., the architect/builder of the new facility; Harry Ecker, AET '71, president of the student council; and John Rich, chairman of the board at Wentworth.

The seal of the newly founded College. Its name was carefully considered; the two magic words, "of Technology" carried great weight in the higher education milieu that Wentworth aspired to join.

Opinions about the College split in two camps. The trustees supported Beatty's reasoning: a market had begun to emerge in the workplace for baccalaureate-level technical graduates. In the workplace, Beatty argued, a harmful gap had developed between professional engineers, who studied for five years, and engineering technicians, who studied for two years. The College-educated engineering technologist could bridge that gap.

What's more, the new College wouldn't have to work too hard to find enrollees—the two-year Institute offered a ready-made breeding ground. And the economics were persuasive: student turnover would occur at a less dizzying pace and Wentworth would receive four years of tuition income rather than two.

Many members of the extended Wentworth family, however, were less enamored with the idea of Wentworth College of Technology. These dissenters saw the College as an abandonment of the Institute's core philosophy, an unneeded escalation, a taking-on of airs. Many thousands of young men, they argued, had thrived in their careers after studying for two years at Wentworth Institute. Was this not good enough anymore?

Beatty, conscious of the shaky support for this major decision, kept few people on campus in the planning loop. In fact, when Beatty finally announced the establishment of the College in 1969, he gave it as a scoop to the student newspaper, Wenitech. (The news came as a surprise to the faculty of Wentworth Institute, and probably added motive to the teachers' decision to unionize in 1973.)

The College started slowly. The first class in 1970 consisted of 113 students; the following year another 140 signed on, bringing the total enrollment to 250.

For the first few years, Wentworth College of Technology offered bachelor of science degrees in architectural, civil, electronic, management, and mechanical engineering technology. Henry Poydar, dean of the college, wrote in 1972: "This is an applied engineering degree. Our goal is to turn out engineering technologists, who are primarily applications oriented, but who also have a sound background in the theoretical aspects of engineering."

The dean continued with an important distinction: "Most people tend to place the engineering technologist somewhere between the engineering technician and the engineer. This is wrong. The degree we grant is not just a bachelor of engineering technology, but rather a bachelor of *science* in engineering technology. This means that while our solutions to engineering problems are hardware-oriented, the basic concepts are also highly stressed. The Wentworth College of Technology graduate is an applied engineer and must take his rightful place beside the science-oriented engineers from other colleges and universities."

Over the next three decades, that's exactly what he, and she, would do.

15 Great Days IN WENTWORTH HISTORY

As of April 5, 2004, Wentworth Institute of Technology has seen 36,525 days come and go. Some of these have been especially sweet ones for the school. Here's a look at 15 red-letter days in the Institute's historical calendar.

Right: An excerpt from the November 17, 1908, deed that established Wentworth Institute on the corner of Huntington Avenue and Ruggles Street. The value of the land has appreciated by a factor of 500 during the past 96 years.

Right: President William H. Taft, at 330 pounds, was perhaps more famous for the size of his White House bathtub than for the impact of his policies.

1. DIRECTORS PURCHASE LAND
(NOVEMBER 17, 1908)

Four-and-a-half years after Arioch Wentworth's will was entered into the record, seven Institute trustees, led by Paul B. Watson, purchased two tracts of land at Huntington Avenue and Ruggles Street. The first, a 140,000-square-foot triangular lot at the corner of Huntington and Ruggles, is today the site of Sweeney Field. The second, a 359,000-square-foot lot, represents the bulk of today's campus proper. The directors bought the land from the Sewall & Day Cordage Company, a rope manufacturer on Parker Street that outfitted clipper ships during the 19th century. The land cost $446,500, or 16 percent of the founder's bequest. Its value today is approximately $224 million.

2. FORMER PRESIDENT WILLIAM H. TAFT DELIVERS COMMENCEMENT SPEECH
(JUNE 10, 1915)

In just the fourth commencement held at the fledgling Wentworth Institute, 199 young men assembled on campus to receive their hard-earned certificates of graduation. Delivering the address to them was a man only two-and-a-half years removed from the Oval Office, former President William Howard Taft. At the time he visited Wentworth, Taft taught law at Yale University. (In 1920 he became the only former president to sit on the Supreme Court.) He had been persuaded to speak by his old friend and colleague, John Davis Long, who chaired Wentworth's board. The two men had been Cabinet members at the turn of the century: Long as Secretary of Navy under President McKinley, Taft as Secretary of War under President Roosevelt. At Wentworth, Taft chose to address a topic relevant to most of the graduates: the policies adopted by labor unions. While generally in favor of unions, Taft decried their insistence on closed shops: "I think this is a narrow policy and one which ought not to be encouraged by employers. Every man should have the right to earn his living as he will, and if he is not able to see the advantage there is in the labor union, he must be permitted to work out his own salvation....Certainly the union would be most unreasonable if it did not welcome the accession to the ranks of skilled workmen of such worthy persons as the graduates of this school." Taft's speech merited front-page coverage in all the Boston newspapers the next day—a tremendous splash of publicity for an institution still introducing itself to the region.

3. 101ST ENGINEERS DEMOBILIZE
(APRIL 28, 1919)

Wentworth Institute felt a paternal bond with the 101st Regiment of Engineers that fought in World War I. And for good reason. For one thing, 20 Wentworth alumni served in its ranks. More than that, though, the Institute had provided technical training to the entire Regiment for four months in 1917 before its cadets shipped overseas to serve in the Great War. While at Wentworth, they took intensive courses in practical military engineering. They slept in tents pitched on what is today Sweeney Field, and ate in mess tents stationed where Watson Hall stands today. On September 26, 1917, the Regiment departed Wentworth and sailed for France as part of the 26th Division. They stayed overseas for 579 days—digging trenches, building bridges, laying rail, constructing hospitals, and carrying out countless other responsibilities. When Uncle Sam called the 101st Engineers home on April 28, 1919, Principal Arthur Williston wrote that Wentworth Institute felt like "a father welcoming home 1,700 sons."

Above and right: Wentworth Institute instructed the 101st Engineers and several other detachments of Army and Navy recruits in eight- and sixteen-week training intervals. Before shipping overseas, members from each detachment received certificates at ceremonies held in front of the Main Building.

Sinclair Weeks Sr. chaired the board for 19 years, the longest service in Wentworth history.

4. SINCLAIR WEEKS SR. JOINS THE BOARD
(FEBRUARY 20, 1928)

Continuity is a precious asset for an institution such as Wentworth Institute of Technology. And two men named Weeks have provided it more conspicuously than anyone else in school history. Sinclair Weeks Sr. was mayor of the city of Newton, Mass., when he joined Wentworth Institute's board of directors in 1928. It marked the first of 76 consecutive years that he and/or his son would sit on the board. The elder Weeks built an illustrious career of public service. He served as a U.S. Senator and then as President Dwight Eisenhower's Secretary of Commerce from 1953 to 1958. 1953 also marked the year he was elected chairman of Wentworth's board, a position he held for the next 19 years—the longest term in the school's history. One of his most able colleagues on the board was his son, Sinclair Weeks Jr., who joined in 1951 and remains a trustee to this day. In one of his first official duties, he brought the name of H. Russell Beatty to the board's presidential search committee. A longtime chairman of the Reed and Barton Corporation, Weeks has served 53 years on the board, a tenure that ranks second only to Kenrick Baker's 55 years. Five of these years—from 1976 to 1981—he spent as chairman. Most important, though, he and his father forged—at the highest ranks—a chain of institutional memory that has helped keep intact the most admirable qualities from Wentworth's early decades.

For more than 60 years, students have disembarked from the Green Line trolley at 8 a.m. and crossed Huntington Avenue to begin the school day.

5. HUNTINGTON AVENUE SUBWAY LINE OPENS
(FEBRUARY 6, 1941)

Not until Wentworth Institute of Technology's 97th year, 2001-02, did more of its students live on campus than commute to and from it. Indeed, Wentworth cut its teeth as a commuter school and thrived for the entire 20th century as just that. Public transportation played a key part in making that a workable arrangement for the Institute. Of course, students driving their automobiles to Wentworth became ever more popular starting in the early 1950s. But carving out enough parking spaces in the middle of a busy city block quickly proved a finite proposition. That left the streetcar stop 100 yards up Huntington Avenue—today part of the MBTA's Green Line—as the means by which thousands of students over the years have arrived at Wentworth's front door.

6. GI Bill Enacted Into Law

(JUNE 22, 1944)

Ed O'Leary, AC '48, one of many Wentworth alumni who took advantage of the GI Bill.

A hole exists in Wentworth's history that parallels one felt nationwide. For two years, 1944 and 1945, Wentworth Institute did not educate tuition-paying students. The reason, of course, was that the young men who normally would have been roaming Wentworth's halls were thousands of miles away fighting the Second World War. President Franklin D. Roosevelt sewed a patch for both holes in June 1944 when he signed into law the GI Bill, which subsidized college tuition and related expenses for America's veterans. Over the next decade, close to 1,000 Wentworth men benefited from the bill. For some, it was a just reward for services rendered; for others, it actually provided incentive to gain a college education that otherwise may have passed them by. "I consider it one of the most wonderful pieces of legislation ever passed by the Congress and signed by the president," says Ed O'Leary, AC '48, an Army veteran who served in the China/Burma/India Theater from 1944 to 1946. "For the simple reason that it gave so much momentum to returning veterans. It allowed fellows like me to develop so many skills and such confidence."

7. Russ Beatty Accepts Job as President

(FEBRUARY 18, 1953)

For 18 years, Wentworth Institute was a second family to Dr. H. Russell Beatty. A colleague once described Beatty's operating philosophy as, "If it's good for Wentworth, then I'm all for it." He died of a heart attack in 1972, a short time after retiring as president of Wentworth College of Technology.

The single most important decision made during Wentworth's first 50 years was the hiring of H. Russell Beatty to lead the Institute into its second 50. It's impossible to imagine Wentworth Institute of Technology today absent the influence exerted by Beatty during his 18-year presidency. When he arrived in 1953, the Institute enrolled 569 students, each of whom departed with a certificate in hand. By the time he retired in 1971, Wentworth Institute had matured into an accredited, associate-degree-granting school that enrolled 1,550 students, and the baccalaureate-level upper division had taken root, setting the stage for the four-year college, Wentworth Institute of Technology, that would emerge in 1977. The force and the vision behind these crucial transformations was Russ Beatty.

8. Charter Amended to Grant Associate's Degree

(June 29, 1956)

Governor Christian Herter (seated, second from right) welcomed President Beatty (seated, second from left) and a group of Wentworth VIPs to his State House office to sign the amended charter. Several trustees attended, including Sinclair Weeks Sr. (seated, far left) and Jr. (standing, far right); Paul B. Watson Jr. (standing, second from left); and John Volpe, AC '30 (standing, far left). Volpe is staring at a desk he'd occupy four-and-a-half years later.

Weeks after beginning his presidency in 1953, Russ Beatty drafted a memorandum to the board of trustees, detailing the direction he wished Wentworth Institute to take. "I wish to recommend," he wrote, "that we take action to amend our Charter so as to make it possible for Wentworth Institute to grant the junior college degree of associate in applied science to graduates of our accredited technical courses." The newcomer Beatty realized that the ability of a Wentworth graduate to advance in his chosen field was starting to be hampered by what the technical industry called "a lack of recognized credentials." The trend, Beatty advised the trustees, "is definitely toward the use of the associate's degree by technical institutes, and we should be a leader in this movement rather than one of the last to come in." The trustees heeded the president's advice and, three years later, the school's charter was officially amended in Massachusetts Governor Christian Herter's office. In June 1957, Wentworth Institute awarded its first associate in engineering degrees to graduates in a ceremony at Symphony Hall. (The associate in applied science degree arrived two years later.)

A view of the Alumni Library from the mezzanine level of Beatty Hall.

9. Alumni Library Opens

(September 5, 1967)

In the life of any college, there are transitional moments—instances when an institution transforms from one sort to another altogether. For Wentworth, the 1967 opening of the Alumni Library represented such a moment. Prior to 1967, Wentworth's library barely deserved the name. Rather, it was more a ragtag collection of books that hopscotched from one ill-suited location to the next. President H. Russell Beatty, however, had always placed a high priority on developing a respectable library. In his first report to the directors in 1954, he wrote: "Good schools have good libraries. When dreamers dream of fine educational institutions, they see buildings, teachers, and students, but above all a fine library to breathe life into minds, to kindle inspiration in youth, to implement classroom learning with a broad spectrum of supplementary information." When the Alumni Library, with a healthy 22,000-volume collection, finally opened 13 years later in the newly constructed

Above and right: A college library proves the axiom that knowledge is dynamic. Even in an age of proliferating digital media, the number of volumes carried by Wentworth's Alumni Library has grown from 22,000 in 1967 to 70,000 today.

In 1977, the Institute feted the members (shown here with their families) of the graduating class of mechanical engineering technology. These 28 young men, over the course of two hard-working semesters, bore witness to the viability of cooperative education at Wentworth Institute of Technology.

Beatty Hall, it demonstrated the Institute's eagerness to raise its profile and meet the standards set by accrediting agencies. As a result, the library's arrival helped the school clear one of the highest hurdles in its path toward the introduction three years later of the baccalaureate-level Wentworth College of Technology.

10. Students Punch Clock on First Co-op Job

(September 3, 1975)

Thirty years ago, a few dozen colleges in the country employed cooperative education—a model of learning in which students integrate paid work experience with classroom instruction. Then, in 1975, co-op found one of its greatest champions in Wentworth. That September, 28 members of the mechanical engineering technology class of 1977 began their four-month work assignments. The jobs these "guinea pigs" worked that semester were challenging—such as a draftsman at the National Park Service, a machinist at Vulcan Tool Manufacturing, and an engineering technician at the Veterans Administration Hospital. When the semester ended, Wentworth knew that co-op fit well into its curriculum. To this day, the program remains Wentworth's crown jewel.

Coach Frank Nestor in the huddle with his basketball team. In Nestor's opinion, the finest basketball game his Leopards ever played was a narrow loss to the Canadian National team at the Canadian Classic tournament in January 1990. "Those Wentworth kids were ferocious," said the National Team coach after the game.

11. Wentworth Joins the NCAA
(September 4, 1984)

When Professor Frank Nestor agreed to succeed Carl Swanson as dean of student affairs in 1983, he did so on one condition. The longtime basketball coach asked President Ted Kirkpatrick for permission to pursue an initiative close to his heart. Wentworth's entry into the National Collegiate Athletic Association was long overdue, Nestor argued. "Our kids deserved it," he said. "It was the only way to bring athletics to the level where it deserved to be at Wentworth. If our teams wanted to join a conference, for example, we needed to be part of the NCAA." The Institute's admission into the NCAA, however, may have been most significant on an emblematic level. It offered unmistakable evidence of Wentworth's arrival as a fully developed four-year college. So, on November 21, 1987, when Coach Nestor's NCAA-level basketball team traveled to Cambridge and upset MIT, it may not have affected league standings very much, but the sheer symbolism of it spoke volumes.

12. Big Dig Receives Federal Funding
(April 2, 1987)

On April 2, 1987, the U.S. House of Representatives—by the razor-thin margin of one vote—overrode the veto of President Ronald Reagan to provide federal funding for what was being called "an interesting little highway project up in Boston." The vote ended up putting tens of millions of dollars in the pockets of hard-working Wentworth alumni. Over the past decade, Boston's Central Artery/Tunnel project, known as the Big Dig, has sparked countless opinions pro and con. But while some critics call it a boondoggle, Wentworth alumni call it a godsend. Hundreds of graduates have worked on this job, the largest highway project ever carried out. Over the course of its 13 years, the Big Dig offered abundant employment opportunities for virtually every major offered at Wentworth—whether it be mechanical engineering technology, construction management, or architectural engineering technology.

You could fill Watson Auditorium several times over with the number of Wentworth graduates who have worked on Boston's $16-billion Central Artery/Tunnel project.

Above: Two architecture projects from 1991. Today, Wentworth's bachelor of architecture curriculum is the only daytime undergraduate professional degree program in Massachusetts to have gained approval from the National Architectural Accrediting Board.

Below: The renovated architecture studio, early 1990s.

13. Architecture Program Earns NAAB Accreditation

(January 1, 1992)

A major steppingstone in Wentworth's maturation as a first-rate baccalaureate teaching institution was its decision to offer the bachelor of architecture degree program. At first glance, it seemed a detour from the school's traditional teaching path. The Institute's trademark had long been engineering technology, which is characterized by a teaching philosophy that doesn't mix all that easily with the requirements of a professional degree program. On the other hand, Wentworth historically had shown great flexibility in tailoring its curriculum as well as a willingness to build on its strengths. So, the Institute listened carefully in the '80s when the registration board for architects came to Wentworth with a proposal for establishing a professional degree program. In the late 1970s, the marketplace had made clear the need for such a program; the industry was pushing more and more for graduates to become registered professionals. "We had a good foundation upon which to build," says Provost George Balich, himself a registered architect. "We had interested students and a qualified, capable faculty who understood the marketplace." The provost at the time, Arthur Thompson, pushed for changes to the charter that would enable the program to be offered. Next, the Institute made a major investment in facility upgrades, spending a million dollars in 1991 to build a studio on the third floor of the Annex building. Finally, in 1992, Wentworth Institute of Technology received retroactive accreditation from the National Architectural Accrediting Board, academia's equivalent of the Good Housekeeping seal of approval. The program has been one of Wentworth's most successful ever since.

Sweeney Field, as it looked on the morning it opened, October 5, 1996. It has provided the Leopards an unmistakable home field advantage. In the past seven years, the men's lacrosse and men's and women's soccer teams have won 70 percent of the games they've played at Sweeney.

14. MYLES SWEENEY TELEPHONES DICK BURTT
(JANUARY 5, 1993)

During the past couple of decades, philanthropic alumni have played an increasingly crucial role in sustaining the excellence of colleges and universities nationwide. On January 5, 1993, Dick Burtt, Wentworth's vice president for development, answered a phone call that introduced him to the alumnus who would set a new standard for philanthropic support of Wentworth. One year after that phone call, Myles Sweeney, AC '28, and his wife, Eugenia, donated two million dollars worth of land to Wentworth. The Institute used the proceeds to build its showpiece athletic field on the corner of Huntington Avenue and Ruggles Street. Sweeney was an old-guard alumnus who bankrolled his alma mater for two fundamental reasons: one, he appreciated what the Institute meant to his own career; and two, he liked what he saw in the modern-day Wentworth Institute of Technology. It is precisely this dynamic that drives the fund raising that will help keep Wentworth in top form well into the 21st century.

15. CANDICE LEE REYNOLDS GRADUATES
(MAY 21, 1995)

When Susan Hardt graduated in 1974, the entire auditorium erupted in applause to honor her accomplishment as Wentworth's first woman graduate. When Candice Lee Reynolds walked on stage to receive her bachelor of architecture degree in 1995, her family and a few friends applauded. That's only because no one at the time realized that she had just become the 1,000th woman to graduate from Wentworth Institute of Technology. History tells us that her accomplishment deserved as much applause as Hardt's. Because she had been the trailblazer, Sue Hardt symbolized women as the exception at Wentworth. Candice Lee Reynolds, on the other hand, represented something far more important: women as the norm.

1971

1990

THE KIRKPATRICK ERA, 1971-1990

Top left: Dr. Edward T. Kirkpatrick, Wentworth's second president.

Left: The 1983 acquisition of the Annex Building, formerly Boston Trade High School, allowed Wentworth to accommodate the surging enrollments of the early '80s.

Below: Professor Donald Nickerson, right, teaches civil engineering technology students how to operate a transit, 1984. Nickerson taught at Wentworth from 1970 to 1993; his excellence as a structural engineer was matched only by the dishevelment of his appearance.

Edward T. ("Ted") Kirkpatrick was Wentworth Institute of Technology's second president. He arrived in 1971 and ended up serving a year longer than had his legendary predecessor, H. Russell Beatty. And when Kirkpatrick retired in 1990, he left behind a legacy just as full as Beatty's.

The trustees of Wentworth Institute considered themselves lucky to find Dr. Kirkpatrick. A 46-year-old dean of the College of Engineering at Rochester Institute of Technology, he also had industrial experience as a mechanical engineer.

But the ace up this candidate's sleeve, the trustees believed, was his unique experience at RIT dealing with a circumstance similar to one that Wentworth seemed likely to face in the near future. Kirkpatrick, you see, had been integral in the successful relocation of the entire RIT campus from one site in Rochester to another miles away.

Wentworth's trustees took close note of this experience because a proposal was gaining steam in Boston to build the "Inner Belt," an eight-lane highway from the South End to Somerville that would connect the radial highways that loop around the city. Although a fascinating idea from an urban planning perspective, it presented a potentially fatal prospect for Wentworth, since the main part of its campus lay smack in the crosshairs of land that the Highway Department would reclaim by eminent domain. In other words, the Inner Belt's arrival in Boston would ensure Wentworth's departure from the city.

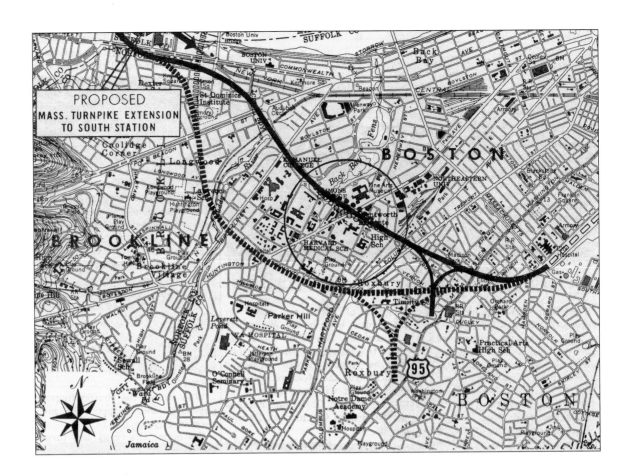

Top: The solid line on this 1960 map shows how the proposed Inner Belt highway would have swallowed up much of the Wentworth campus.

Above: A 1965 rendering of the Inner Belt depicts the eight-lane highway as it enters a tunnel near the Boston University Bridge at the Charles River.

If that happened, the trustees banked on one contingency plan: to relocate operations of the entire school to the Plainville campus in southeastern Massachusetts. And perhaps only one or two men on the planet knew more about transplanting a college campus than Ted Kirkpatrick. (As it turned out, the Inner Belt proposal collapsed of its own weight in the early '70s, frustrating future generations of urban commuters, but causing anyone connected with Wentworth to breathe an enormous sigh of relief.)

Ted Kirkpatrick took over as president of Wentworth Institute in July 1971. Meanwhile, Russ Beatty retained the presidency of the year-old Wentworth College of Technology. This co-presidency lasted less than a year, however. On June 30, 1972, Dr. Beatty retired from the College; three months later he died. After Beatty's death, the trustees assigned Kirkpatrick to head both the lower and upper divisions of Wentworth. He brought significant change to each during the next few years.

In Wentworth's history, there exists no five-year stretch more eventful than the 1972-1977 phase at the start of the Kirkpatrick era. In that span, the president enacted three enormous changes at Wentworth.

WENTWORTH WELCOMES WOMEN

Above right: President Kirkpatrick greets four of the first five women who enrolled at Wentworth Institute in the fall of 1972. From left: Doris Dennis; Jane Estella, AET '75; Virginia Butcher, AET '75; and Deborah Banks, AET '75. The fifth, not pictured, was Sue Hardt, BCS '74.

Above: One year later, the female enrollment increased by 160 percent. President Kirkpatrick posed on the front steps of Wentworth Hall with nine of the 13 women who entered Wentworth in September 1973. This photo op marked the last time these young women represented a majority on the campus. Once classes started, men outnumbered them 143 to 1.

The first was coeducation. Sometimes it takes an outsider to see the obvious. The day he arrived on the Wentworth campus, Kirkpatrick said, "My initial thought was, 'Where are the women?' I just couldn't fathom that in this day and age a school could still be all male. It happened that only a few weeks later I had to fill out some government forms justifying the single-sex enrollment at the school. In fact, I couldn't justify it. I sent back the forms saying that it was my hope Wentworth would become coeducational very soon."

First, the president needed to persuade the board of trustees that it was a good move to make. This took some work. The board, made up of 18 men, was a conservative group. Progressive these trustees were not. Kirkpatrick said, "Previously, the board had informed me…that they saw no need to provide a technical education for women, especially when there were women's colleges, Emmanuel and Simmons, just down the street."

By April 1972, however, Kirkpatrick had made his case convincingly. On the 20th of that month, the trustees accepted and ratified the recommendation of the board's education committee that women be admitted to Wentworth.

Perhaps the board simply resorted to a cost-benefit analysis. In other words, the cost to build a few ladies' restrooms seemed cheap indeed when weighed against the prospect of doubling the number of tuition-paying students to whom the school might offer its services.

In truth, no one at the Institute held such lofty expectations for the enrollment of women. As the administration wrote in 1972, "We at Wentworth are not anticipating droves of women applying for admission, at least not for this academic year."

And were they ever right. A mere five women entered the grounds of Wentworth Institute in the fall of 1972 to meet their 2,500 male classmates. They

BETWEEN US GIRLS

Girls, well I'm glad to see our population has doubled this year. I guess you've already heard or discovered for yourselves the problems of finding a ladies' room in Mickelson Hall, or the disadvantages of walking down Huntington Ave. with a hard hat and steel-tipped shoes, so I won't discuss them at length. What I will try to do is give you a few hints.

Do not, if you are lucky enough to take the course, be discouraged by Building Materials, more fondly called "Mud Lab." Let your partner, if he is a he, carry the mortar for you, and you offer to get the bricks. Chances are, after carrying a few loads of brick, you will not even be able to pick up your toothbrush the next morning. But take heart, soon it will be nothing and you'll wonder why the sleeves on your shirt are beginning to fit a little tighter. Also, be prepared to sweat to death and wear something that can afford to get covered in mortar.

Now, concerning Physics Labs; they will be much easier if you simply don't try to figure out the reasoning behind the equations they give you. Just plug in the appropriate numbers and forget about it. Also, do the projects, they will add a few extra points.

I guess there isn't too much else to cover. I want to wish you good luck and a good year. If you have any questions, just contact me through the student files.

Sue Hardt, BCS

(Letter to new female students, Wenitech newspaper, October 12, 1973)

Barbara Wotka, AET '77, AE '79, left, and Constance Perry, AET '77, apply a stress test to their "Mud Lab" masonry project, 1976.

were Virginia Butcher, AET '75; Doris Dennis; Jane Estella, AET '75; Susan Hardt, BCS '74; and Deborah Banks, AET '75.

It's worth noting that, despite extraordinary pressures, 80 percent of this first class of women at Wentworth stayed the course and earned a degree—a graduation rate that far outperformed the school's norm. (Another current-day statistic further emphasizes the merits of the coeducation revolution: Although female students today represent only 18 percent of the student population, they manage to collect 30 percent of the awards presented each year for scholastic achievement.)

Alumnae give mixed accounts of the first few years of coeducation. Trailblazer Sue Hardt offers a positive and good-humored review: "I found the experience of being the first woman graduate anything but traumatic. The men in my building construction major treated me very respectfully. This was fortunate since there was not a single woman in my classes!"

Lisa Connors Chatterjee, CST '77, also enjoyed her time at Wentworth: "I never felt out of place here. Since day one I had the pleasure of feeling right at home. Teachers accepted me for what I was: a student. I did not experience any kind of double standard or prejudice. Sure, there were a few technicalities—

The heart of Wentworth has always been its classrooms and laboratories.

Clockwise from top left: Alvin Page, shown here in 1971, taught architectural engineering technology at Wentworth from 1949 to 1972.

Arthur Nelson instructs a mechanical design lab, 1976.

Machine shop, 1972.

1974 aircraft maintenance technology students give a helicopter the once-over.

such as having only one bathroom in each building, or having to use the First Aid Station as a locker room at the gym. But as far as attitudes and atmosphere, there was never a problem."

The ratio, however, was daunting, says Roxann Arey, CST '77. "I'll admit that until I arrived at Wentworth, I had no idea there would be so few women. That was an eye opener!" And the attitudes that the female students encountered could sometimes be unenlightened. "I'm not asking for instant gentlemen," wrote Virginia Butcher in 1972. "There are few of them anywhere today. All I ask for is the right to wear regular short dresses without being made embarrassed or having to wear shorts underneath them."

As time passed, women became part of the fabric of Wentworth Institute of Technology. In President Kirkpatrick's last year, 1989-90, 437 female students studied at Wentworth, representing 11 percent of the class. By 2002-03, the numbers had risen even more, to 589 students and 18 percent.

Women also began to make their presence felt at the highest levels of the Institute. In 1979, the trustees appointed the first woman to the board, R. Yvonne Park, president of Wes-Pine Millwork.

The hiring of women faculty was perhaps the most difficult challenge at Wentworth. Lois Ascher broke the ice in 1972. But their numbers did not increase as steadily as the administration hoped. Kirkpatrick admitted the problem in 1990: "Our recruitment of women faculty is not as substantial as I'd like to see it. Part of the problem is the limited number of professional women who have the technical background necessary to teach our students. And these candidates are very much in demand." By the 2003-04 academic year, women made up 21 percent of Wentworth's full-time faculty (the administration's goal is 35 percent by 2007).

Granted, there probably never will be parity between the number of men and women in Wentworth's student body. Engineering and engineering technology programs nationwide max out at 25-to-30 percent women. Socio-cultural biases play a big part in this disparity: to this day, for instance, the general public continues to regard the idea of a female construction worker with a certain apprehension.

Far left: By 1989, women made up 11 percent of the full-time enrollment at Wentworth Institute of Technology.

Left: It took several years for varsity sports to be offered to women. In the meantime, several students took it upon themselves to organize a cheerleading squad in 1976. Clockwise from back left: Ellen Walsh, CST '77; Diane Murphy, AET '78; Constance Perry, AET '77; and Debbie Bezanson, AET '77.

Nineteen members of the mechanical engineering technology class of 1977, the pioneers of cooperative education at Wentworth. Seated, left to right: Charles Barron, Peter Paciorek, Dewey Glick, Edward Boudreau, Paul McManus, James Reidy, William Connell, and Bradford Heil. Standing, left to right: Mark Thomas, Neal Madden, David Black, Steven Johnson, Matthew Curran, Real Poirier, Robert Spaulding, Omar Salameh, Joseph Rock, Eliot Weisman, and Herbert Speck.

CO-OP: THE CROWN JEWEL

Cooperative education was the second major advance of President Kirkpatrick's first few years. The concept was fairly well known. A number of colleges and universities in North America had incorporated co-op into their curricula since its introduction at the University of Cincinnati in 1905. Kirkpatrick happened to be well acquainted with the program: he had seen it in action for many years at Rochester Institute of Technology. Plus, his new next-door neighbor, Northeastern University, had enjoyed great success with cooperative education.

Co-op, which supplements traditional classroom and laboratory instruction with semesters of professional, paid work experience, seemed a great fit for Wentworth. The same practical, hands-on philosophy that underpins cooperative education had always been a fundamental characteristic of the Institute, dating back 142 years to the day when 20-year-old Arioch Wentworth turned his back on studying law at Dartmouth College, and chose instead to journey to Boston and learn the soapstone trade from the ground up.

The only reason cooperative education didn't appear at Wentworth until 1975 was because the program only made sense at a four-year school. But, with the upper-division College up and running for five years, co-op's time at Wentworth had arrived.

From 1973 to 1975, Charlie Pheeney, director of development, secured three grants totaling $48,000 to research and implement a cooperative education program at Wentworth.

The guinea pigs turned out to be 27 mechanical engineering technology students who entered Wentworth College in 1975. These young men worked their first co-op assignments in the Spring 1976 semester. Paul Mullen, for instance, worked as a machine operator at Quinzani's Bakery. Real Poirier was a draftsman for the National Park Service. Ali Zariv stayed close to home—he tended the boiler in the Wentworth Power Plant.

Not every assignment was a success, but most were. This encouraging start gave the administration heart to introduce the co-op program into each of the other majors at the College. By the mid-1980s, co-op had established itself as the crown jewel of Wentworth's curriculum. "When we ask students what drew

Co-op: An In-Depth Experience

When Chris Levy, a 1994 construction management major, took up scuba diving as a youngster, he could hardly have imagined where it would lead him. "But there I was in the fall of 1993 headed for Japan," he says. His mission: underwater inspection of two U.S. naval bases—Yokosuka, about an hour-and-a-half away from Tokyo, and Sasebo, on the southern coast of Kyushu.

"This all came about," explains Levy, "when Childs Engineering Corporation, a Medfield, Mass., marine engineering firm, contacted the Wentworth Co-op Office looking for a civil engineering major with scuba diving experience. My co-op coordinator told me about the opening and I contacted them. Since my major was in the same ballpark, they hired me."

"We'd had good luck with Wentworth students we hired in the past, so it seemed natural to use the school as a resource again," notes Craig Sams, senior design engineer at Childs.

A crew of five from Childs, including Levy, flew to Tokyo as part of the company's ongoing contract with the U.S. Navy to handle underwater inspection of its bases in Japan. The Childs contract is one of many the Navy has entered into with private companies to ensure that U.S. bases are maintained in top-notch condition worldwide.

"Our first task," says Levy, "was to examine the sea-walls that surround the bases for damage from ships, seismic activity, or erosion. I was one of three divers. Two of us handled the underwater inspection, measured the damage, recorded it on camera, and reported the findings to the third diver who stayed topside to record the data. Then we'd rotate positions, so we all got a chance to dive. We looked for chips, cracks, air-holes, or exposed steel rods in the seawall.

"Sometimes I spent five or six hours a day in water that dipped as low as 64 degrees. We wore expensive Viking drysuits, which were very effective because they retain body heat better than wetsuits," explains Levy. "It wasn't easy work. Everything is distorted underwater and, in addition to the camera, we'd descend with a mason's hammer, light, measuring tape, and an ultrasound 'gun' that detected the thickness of the steel reinforcements in the walls. We had to spend hours hacking the marine life from the walls before we could even examine them."

One would think that Levy might have suffered from a case of emotional "bends" when he returned to reality and the States in November 1993, but Childs kept him diving. He went to Philadelphia, again for the Navy, to assist with an underwater inspection of mooring chains on the *Iowa* and *Wisconsin* battleships.

He also worked on two other Childs accounts, conducting an underwater inspection of Mass. Pike bridges, and checking the construction of two new piers that help support condominiums at Battery Wharf on Boston's waterfront.

"This co-op was great," said Levy in 1994. "When I graduate, I'd love to work for a marine engineering firm like Childs. I could make use of my Wentworth education and my favorite hobby. That would be the best of both worlds."

Reprinted from "Sharp Students Land Exciting Jobs," by Patricia Lillis, Wentworth Alumni News, Spring 1994.

[Today, Levy works as a senior project engineer for the Perini Building Company. He's currently working on the construction of a 22-story Marriott hotel at the Adriaen's Landing redevelopment project in Hartford, Conn.]

them to Wentworth," noted Dean of Students Maureen Keefe in 2000, "it's always co-op, co-op, co-op."

Compelling reasons make this so. Chief among them is the fact that two-thirds of Wentworth's graduates each year accept their first full-time job from an employer with whom they had previously worked a co-op semester. And whether or not graduates sign on with a familiar employer, co-op provides them a competitive advantage in the hiring process. Employers in technical and engineering fields are notorious for wanting entry-level job candidates to possess one year of related experience. Co-op experience fits that bill perfectly for Wentworth graduates. Students also point out that lessons and skills learned on co-op jobs add value to the classroom experience because it enables them to absorb their coursework with a more sophisticated perspective. In addition, Wentworth students during the past 28 years have scored some plum co-op assignments. [*See "Co-op: An In-Depth Experience" at left.*]

Co-op's integration into the curriculum only reinforced the Institute's "we work harder" reputation. The two semesters that students had to dedicate to co-op made summer terms necessary so that they could complete their bachelor's degree requirements in four (or, in some cases, five) years.

In the years following Watergate, Wentworth students felt less and less shy about airing their disgruntlement with the "establishment," as this 1979 cartoon attests.

Only At Wentworth

1. Do you spend half an hour looking for a book, and eventually find out that it's been stolen.

2. We have full time employees just to fix the doors. (Which were fixed two days ago.)

3. We have full time employees just to paint the walls (which were painted a week ago).

4. Do we go to the library for some quiet study, and find out students laughing, shouting, talking about their wild weekend.

5. Do we get a juicy burger, but its juicy because they hardly clean the grease from the pen.

6. We have pot holes at the driveways, deep enough for a swim.

7. We have a volleyball field right next to the parked cars.

8. We have bathrooms without any doors.

29. Lois Ascher

The Integrator

The first five women who enrolled at the Institute in the fall of 1972 changed the face of Wentworth forever. But they ended only half of

the school's single sex tradition. Lois Ascher ended the 61-year run of an all-male faculty when she joined the Institute in 1972 to teach English. "It's nice to be unique at something," she said at the time. "When I came to Wentworth, even the instructors stared at me. It was stranger for them than it was for me!" Today, after 32 years and more than 100 female teaching colleagues, Lois Ascher remains one of the most popular professors in Wentworth's Humanities, Social Sciences, and Management Department. A longtime colleague in the department is her husband, Frank Rooney, who has taught English at Wentworth since 1957, one of the longest tenures of any professor in the Institute's history.

30. Rolf E. Davey, AME '55

The Aviator

Since 1950, the American Society for Engineering Education has honored five Wentworth men—including two principals and two presidents—with its esteemed James H. McGraw Award.

Among this elite group, Chuck Davey was the lone alumnus, and also the one who toiled the longest on the front lines of engineering technology education. The aircraft maintenance and aeronautical engineering technology programs that flourished for decades at Wentworth owed much of their success to Davey. A 1955 graduate of the aircraft maintenance program, Davey joined the faculty in 1961 and quickly established himself as the linchpin of the aeronautical program at Wentworth. He taught at Wentworth for 44 years. An avid pilot (a passion he shared with President Ted Kirkpatrick), Davey once donated a plane owned by Arthur Godfrey to the Institute.

31. Arioch Wentworth Erickson Jr.

The Great-Grandson

As a 16-year trustee and chair of the board from 1981 to 1985, Arioch Wentworth Erickson Jr. was

twice blessed. His inclusion on the board derived partly from his bloodlines. His monogram alone spoke volumes: he was the great-grandson of school founder Arioch Wentworth. But Bill Erickson would have been supremely qualified for Wentworth's board even if genetics hadn't been in his favor. A graduate of MIT, where he earned both bachelor's and master's degrees in civil engineering, he started as a field engineer and eventually became president of West India Chemicals Ltd., a solar salt operation in the Bahamas. Erickson's daughter, Louise Ulbrich, served as a corporator until 1998. When she retired, it ended a 94-year tradition of family representation on the Wentworth corporation. Bill Erickson died in January 2002 at the age of 97.

32. Susan Hardt, BCS '74

The Trailblazer

Wentworth couldn't have invented an abler candidate to break the gender barrier than Sue Hardt. One of five young women to enroll at Wentworth Institute in 1972, she alone graduated two years later (the rest followed suit in 1975). The audience embraced the cum laude building construction graduate with a standing ovation when she walked onstage to pick up her diploma at the May 1974 commencement. The applause was partially a response to her uniqueness. More than that, though, it was a sign of respect for a young woman whose courage and determination guided her down a path trodden

for the previous 63 years by 21,399 men, yet not a single woman. A 1975 alumni magazine article paid tribute to her strength, calling her "Woman of Steel." Trailblazing came naturally to her, apparently. In 1978-79, she served as Alumni Association president—the first female ever to hold the position.

33. Frederick "Ted" Hood, BC '50

The Skipper

Life is full of pleasing ironies. First, consider the blue-blood bastion that is yacht racing. Now, consider it being dominated for years by a blue-collar graduate of Wentworth's building construction program. The whole world watched when Ted Hood, BC '50, won the America's Cup yacht race in 1974 aboard *Courageous*. But his legacy extends much further than that one defining race. For the past 50 years, Hood has been a prolific innovator in the sailing industry. He started in 1954 as a sailmaker and was responsible for

advances such as the crosscut spinnaker. His record as a boat designer is beyond compare. Starting with a 14-foot dinghy he built as a 13-year-old in Marblehead, Mass., Hood went on to design and build hundreds of different boats. "I like to do things that haven't been done before," he said in a 1985 interview. "I like to make something better, and be able to prove that it's better." The entire sailing public can attest to his success in this regard.

34. Edward T. Kirkpatrick

The Innovator

Ted Kirkpatrick's first six years as president may have been the most revolutionary period in the school's 100-year history. Arriving in 1971 from

Rochester Institute of Technology, he quickly set in motion three changes that transformed Wentworth. Within a year, he convinced a conservative board of trustees to begin admitting women to Wentworth. Two years later, he rallied a reluctant faculty behind cooperative education, an experiential learning model that has been a full-bodied success ever since. And in 1977, he merged Wentworth Institute with the College of Technology, patiently nurturing a "two-plus-two" philosophy to create a thriving four-year institution. Other accomplishments of Kirkpatrick's tenure included the establishment of a weekend college, the offer of Wentworth's expertise to aid foreign technical schools, and the acquisition of a couple of key properties (the Ira Allen Building and Boston Trade High School). Dr. Kirkpatrick brought the professional instincts of a mechanical engineer to his management of the Institute. For instance, he oversaw the Institute's use of energy with great vigilance and creativity, climaxing in the installation of a 600kW cogeneration unit. Since retiring in 1990, his interests reveal him as a Wentworth man through and through. He earned a degree in aircraft maintenance from East Coast Aero Tech and built a single-wing airplane in the basement of his Weston, Mass., home.

35. Henry C. Lord, MC&TD '13
The Wildcatter

Endowed and term professorships play an important part in sustaining a topnotch college faculty. Half a dozen currently exist at Wentworth Institute of Technology. The concept established its foothold at Wentworth courtesy of a record-setting donation from Henry C. Lord, a graduate of the Institute's second class. In 1979, Lord's estate bequeathed $500,000 to the Institute, at the time the largest gift since Arioch Wentworth's multimillion-dollar donation that founded the school. Lord, a resident of Peterborough, N.H., made his fortune as a wildcatter in the Midwest; he had a talent for finding crude petroleum and natural gasoline in seemingly barren land. His alma mater directed his bequest toward the endowment of a chair in electronic engineering technology. During the past 25 years, the Henry C. Lord Chair has supported the fine work of four Wentworth professors: Alexander Avtgis, IE '58, Frederick Driscoll, Donald Remington, and Robert Villanucci, EEE '66.

36. Leroy S. Olsen
Uncle Leroy

In many respects, Leroy S. Olsen, who taught mechanical engineering technology from 1963 to 1975, stands in for hundreds of men and women

who have taught at Wentworth over the years. He was a professional mechanical engineer with experience in industry and academia; shrewd, tough, and a real character to boot. In two respects, however, Olsen was unique. First, with the founding of Wentworth College in 1970, Olsen became the first faculty member in the school's history to be accorded the title of full professor. President Beatty held him in high regard as a teacher. "If you want a teaching mentor," he told young faculty members, "you need only look at Professor Olsen." The second unique accomplishment was his $1.5-million bequest to Wentworth Institute of Technology, which came to light after Olsen's death in 2002. No employee has ever made a larger gift to the school. Students, however, remember Olsen best for his hardnosed but

compassionate teaching style. He earned the nickname, Uncle Leroy, from the endless procession of students who took part in his informal conferences at the Gold Corner Luncheonette. (A plaque hung in the restaurant: "This table reserved for Leroy Olsen and his ME students.") And colleagues remember a mechanical genius (who had the nerve to improve a classic when he invented his "Leroy Slide Rule"), a world-class spendthrift (who traveled to Norway when he was 63; rather than pay fare at one of the dozens of hotels in the area, he checked into a youth hostel); and a charming friend (Christmas season at Wentworth College didn't officially begin until Leroy had boiled up a batch of his infamous Norwegian concoction known by some as "glug" and others as "paint thinner"—see recipe below).

Olsen's Swedish Punch ("Glug")
1 cup red wine
1 cup sugar
1 dozen whole cloves
3 cinnamon sticks
1 dozen blanched almonds
1/2 cup raisins
1 dozen cardamom seeds (peeled and crushed)

Combine and bring to a boil for 20 minutes. Strain into a jug. Pour whiskey over strainings into jug. Test.

37. Carl Swanson, MW&TM '38
Mr. Wentworth

There's little dispute which individual in the Institute's history merits the nickname, "Mr. Wentworth." No person ever ingratiated himself more deeply into the fabric of Wentworth than did Carl Swanson. Over the span of 48 years, he put his stamp on Wentworth as a student, alumnus, teacher, department head, researcher, dean, and vice president. "Unofficially," said President Edward T. Kirkpatrick, "he was so much more: ambassador to the neighborhood and city, per-

sonal counselor, surrogate parent, arbiter of differences, spokesperson for engineering technology, fund raiser, student advocate, institutional archivist, team player, and champion of the highest standards of human behavior." After graduating in

1938 with a certificate in machine work and tool making, Swanson immediately went to work as an assistant instructor in the Institute's Machine Processes Department. Four years later, with

World War II underway, he ran the machine shop and helped instruct 10,000 Navy recruits destined to become diesel mechanics, machinist's mates, and metal fabricators. For the three decades following the war, Swanson progressed through a series of jobs at Wentworth, including director of special programs and dean of the evening school. He also played a part in research activities through Air Force Contracts; for years he supervised the mechanical development of rocket and balloon instrumentation. But his appointment in 1974 as dean of students, and later vice president of student affairs, made him truly indispensable to President Kirkpatrick. "His tireless devotion, his sense of excitement and initiative, his genuine caring, warmth, and compassion," said Kirkpatrick, "made Carl Swanson an example of the very finest our way of life can produce." Mr. Wentworth, indisputably.

38. Arthur Thompson
The Provost

Arthur Thompson came to Wentworth Institute of Technology in 1979 after a long career as the dean of engineering and vice president/director of Boston University's Europe program. President Kirkpatrick asked him to become chief academic

officer, and later called it one of the best moves he ever made. As provost, Thompson instilled an academic rigor that was new to the Institute, and rewrote the charter to set the stage for the school Wentworth would become in the

'90s. He oversaw the initial accreditation of the upper division, reorganized the academic division into a more collegiate structure, started the weekend college, and introduced professional programs such as civil engineering and architecture. He's also noteworthy for the recommendation he made as trustee and chair of the search committee to find the third president of Wentworth Institute of Technology. Thompson, who also served as a trustee of Norwich University, informed his Wentworth colleagues about a dean there who had an excellent reputation as a teacher and administrator. The candidate's name was John Van Domelen.

Transplanting the "Wentworth Way" Overseas

Ted Kirkpatrick believed so strongly in the Wentworth model of engineering technology education that he took advantage of every opportunity to transplant it overseas.

Wentworth actually enjoyed a long history of service to other nations. The Ford Foundation had hired Principal Frederick Dobbs in the '50s to replicate Wentworth's style of education in Pakistan and India. And in 1962, President H. Russell Beatty had allied Wentworth with the newly founded University of Petroleum and Minerals in Saudi Arabia.

After Dr. Kirkpatrick took charge at Wentworth in 1971, he soon developed a special predilection for foreign programs. He got his feet wet by chairing the consortium that guided the growth of the University of Petroleum and Minerals. Later, institutions in Kuwait, Algeria, and China all benefited from the influence of Wentworth and Kirkpatrick.

The most promising alliance of all was with Shiraz Technical Institute in Iran. In the mid-1970s, Wentworth's best-in-class reputation placed it at the head of the list of institutional mentors for STI. Wentworth consulted on constructing the campus, developing the curriculum, and training the faculty.

For several years, the affiliation yielded great benefits not only for Shiraz Technical Institute, but also for Wentworth and the state economy. A number of Wentworth professors spent a year or two in Shiraz. And the construction of STI and its laboratories pumped into Massachusetts more than a million dollars per year, during what were lean economic times.

Unfortunately, Shiraz Technical Institute met a quick and merciless end when revolution struck Iran in late 1978 and the shah was deposed.

More often, though, Kirkpatrick's and Wentworth's involvement with foreign programs led to happy ends. One such occasion happened during a 1985 consulting visit to the Nakuru Institute of Technology in Kenya, where Ted and his wife, Barbara, were distressed to note the absence of a library. Remedying this through official channels, President Kirkpatrick realized, would yield only a sea of red tape. So he decided to take a detour. Upon returning home, he and Barbara initiated a book drive, asking Wentworth employees to contribute any unwanted volumes, especially textbooks, from their personal collections. Within a couple of weeks, Wentworth shipped a full ton of books overseas—no longer would Nakuru Institute of Technology be without a library.

The consummate host, President Kirkpatrick made Arab students feel right at home when they visited the campus in 1977.

In 1976, Iranian educators completed training at Wentworth to qualify for faculty positions at Shiraz Technical Institute.

The Merger

Top: A clever logotype reinforced the "two-plus-two" curriculum that reigned at Wentworth during the '70s and '80s.

Above: The 1977 seal that heralded the arrival of Wentworth Institute of Technology.

The third major advance in the early years of the Kirkpatrick era was more evolution than revolution. In 1977, Wentworth Institute and Wentworth College of Technology merged into a new corporation called Wentworth Institute of Technology. The merger actually marked the normal maturation of a process that began when the upper-division College first arrived in 1970. For several years, Wentworth had marketed to its students an arrangement called the "two-plus-two" model: Enter the Institute and either leave after two years with an associate's degree, or proceed to the College and pursue a bachelor's degree. By 1977, the redundancies inherent in this structure of two separate-but-related entities made it clear that the time had come for the Institute and College to unite.

The merger carried some risk. A major reason the trustees had operated the College independently was because they assumed it would earn accreditation more easily if it didn't have to carry the baggage of a two-year school. Nevertheless, by 1977 the administration reasoned that the benefits of a merger outweighed the risks.

The same "two-plus-two" philosophy still prevailed at Wentworth. Now, however, it simply happened under one roof instead of two.

The merger represented a watershed moment for alumni—an event that identified to what notion of Wentworth one subscribed. Some alumni worried that the Wentworth that had molded them was getting tossed aside. Other alumni, however, many of whom had gone on to other schools to earn bachelor's degrees, adopted the attitude of, "Times change, so why shouldn't my alma mater?"

The merger also caused some faculty members to scan their CVs nervously. The general rule of thumb was that a professor's terminal degree should be at least one level above the highest degree offered at the school. In 1977, however, only 63 of 133 faculty members (47 percent) held master's degrees, and just three professors held doctorates. Because these statistics matter to accreditors, enhancing the professional development of the faculty became a priority for the administration during the next 25 years. The effort paid off. Today, 99 percent of Wentworth's full-time faculty members hold master's degrees and 31 percent have doctorates.

Wentworth has always been first and foremost a teaching institution. Its professors have rarely been research stars, or prolific authors, or media darlings. They teach, and happen to do it very well. Since day one, the Institute has been only as strong as its teaching staff.

All of these facts made the 1977 faculty strike especially upsetting. That fall, 117 Wentworth professors stayed out of work, picketing the campus and forcing classes to shut down for two weeks.

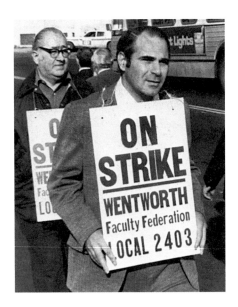

Above: The 1977-78 academic year was the most
turbulent in Wentworth history. Not only did the
faculty strike shut down classes for two weeks in
October, the legendary Blizzard of '78 knocked
classes offline for another full week in February.

The discord had been building for years. Wentworth instructors, in comparison to peers at other institutions, were overworked and undercompensated. In
1971, President Kirkpatrick attended his first faculty meeting and commented
that the instructors were underpaid by an average of $2,000. Unfortunately,
the remedy for this inequity was slow in coming, partly because of a nationwide wage freeze ordered by President Richard Nixon. The faculty also chafed
under heavy teaching loads.

In September 1973, by a thin margin, Wentworth's faculty voted to unionize.
Since that time, they have bargained collectively as members of the American
Federation of Teachers, Local 2403. It was an unusual step to take; of the 2,300
private institutions of higher education in the U.S., only 67 have faculty who
are represented by unions.

The union's entry into the academy pleased neither President Kirkpatrick nor
the trustees. Not only was it uncollegial, they felt, it also hampered the administration's power to reward star performers in the teaching ranks.

The two sides grudgingly hammered out a two-year contract agreement in
1975, but the worst came to bear in the next round of negotiations. On
October 28, 1977, after five months comprising 28 bargaining sessions, followed by one month of federal mediation, the professors hoisted picket signs
and circled the campus. The impasse lasted for 14 days.

Soaring Enrollments, Expanding Campus

Jarring though the strike was, eventually life returned to normal at Wentworth Institute of Technology. By the late '70s and early '80s, Wentworth's campus had changed dramatically from Kirkpatrick's first days at the Institute.

Enrollments were soaring. In 1972, 1,765 day students enrolled at Wentworth. By 1985, the number had nearly doubled to 3,258. For several years in the 1980s, in fact, Wentworth Institute of Technology led the nation in engineering technology enrollment and degrees produced.

Part of that spike was a result of the Institute improving its outreach to working men and women. Since the day it opened in 1911, Wentworth had educated tens of thousands of students in its night school. In 1981, the Institute expanded its offerings to include a weekend college. It has been a staple of Wentworth's continuing education efforts ever since.

The makeup of the daytime student body also played a huge role in causing enrollments to mushroom. Diversity reached Wentworth in the late 1970s. Minority students had enrolled at Wentworth since classes began in 1911, but for more than 60 years the numbers remained low. During H. Russell Beatty's 18 years as president, less than 100 minority students graduated from Wentworth Institute. In 1966, for instance, 790 young men earned degrees; seven of these graduates were minorities. By 1980, these numbers had increased tenfold. And by President Kirkpatrick's last year, 1990, minority students represented 15 percent of the class.

Above: Wentworth doesn't shut down at 5 p.m.; professional and continuing studies have always been an important part of the educational package. Bob Makowiecki, BDEM '02, is one of the 3,000 men and women who've graduated from the Institute's evening and weekend degree programs. By day, he worked as a mechanical engineer at Varian, customizing million-dollar equipment. By night, he earned his bachelor's degree in design engineering (mechanical concentration) at Wentworth. "Education is like having a workshop stocked with tools," says Makowiecki. "You may not always use those tools but you can access them when you need them."

Right: As enrollments grew, so did the size of commencements. Beginning in 1981, graduation ceremonies returned to the Wentworth campus. For many years before that, they had been held off campus at sites such as Symphony Hall and the Hynes Auditorium.

Above: 1987 computer laboratory.

Just as the students were changing, so were the classrooms and laboratories. Computerization prevailed during the Kirkpatrick era. Virtually every laboratory in every discipline taught at Wentworth required the integration of a computerized component. The Institute accomplished this at significant cost. To this day, the same challenge looms constantly over the school. In 2001, for instance, Wentworth spent $1.5 million to bolster its information technology infrastructure. It's the nature of technology not to be static, and it's the nature of students not to accept yesterday's technology. As a result, Wentworth Institute of Technology has always endeavored to stay out in front of a moving, and usually expensive, target.

During the '70s and '80s, the curricular circle of life continued as it always had at the Institute: certain majors died (material science, nuclear engineering technology, welding technology) and new majors (facilities management, interior design, architecture) sprung up in their places.

By the early 1980s, space had become a pressing problem at the Institute. As enrollments climbed higher and higher, Wentworth's core of nine buildings clustered around the quadrangle no longer seemed sufficient to accommodate the instructional and recreational needs of close to 4,000 students.

New construction wasn't in the cards, but the trustees and Kirkpatrick found a resourceful way to solve the problem. The solution was across the street. On Parker Street sat two vacant school buildings owned by the city. One was the Ira Allen Building, a grade school built at the turn of the century. The other had been home to Boston Trade High School from 1915 to 1978. Each facility required significant renovation, but combined they would provide a sorely needed 182,000 square feet to Wentworth's physical plant.

The negotiation for the two properties was handled ingeniously. In lieu of paying cash, Wentworth promised 13 tuition-free scholarships per year to Boston students. The city accepted the offer, and the Institute began to rehabilitate the buildings. By 1984, Wentworth students started crossing Parker Street to take classes. Today, Ira Allen is home to the Applied Mathematics and Sciences Department, and its neighbor, now called the Annex, houses Wentworth's Design and Facilities, Architecture, and Civil, Construction, and Environment Departments.

In the other major building project of the 1980s, the Institute renovated its Evans Way residence hall in 1987. (These apartment buildings next to Tudbury Hall had been purchased in 1967 from alumnus Kenneth Rodgers, MC&TD '36, who was the son of instructor Leigh Rodgers.) Although commuter students still held sway at the Institute, on-campus housing took on a greater profile starting in the early '70s. Baker Hall, with 282 beds, opened on the west corner of campus in 1972. And Edwards/Rodgers Hall has housed 200-plus students each year since being purchased by Wentworth in 1966. (Previously, it was an apartment complex populated by working-class families.)

Above: The Annex is the largest building on the Wentworth campus dedicated entirely to academics.

Right: A 1988 view of the Evans Way housing complex. Today, it offers the first taste of campus living for many members of Wentworth's freshman class.

In January 1990, Wentworth installed a 600kW cogeneration unit in its Power Plant. Running on natural gas, the cogenerator produces:

• two-thirds of the electricity needed for the main campus during summer months;
• 200 tons of steam to power the chiller plant in the summer;
• steam for heat during the winter, allowing the Institute to sell power back to the utility;
• enough backup power to allow the school to stay open during "brown-out" conditions.

IN 1984, WENTWORTH PURCHASED VACANT PROPERTIES ON PARKER, HALLECK, AND PRENTISS STREETS. THE BUILDINGS ONCE FORMED THE HUB OF BOSTON BREWING ACTIVITY IN THE 19TH CENTURY. THE BURKHARDT BREWERY WAS, AT THE TIME, ONE OF THE LARGEST BREWERS IN THE NORTHEAST.

Aircraft instruction had a place at Wentworth for 65 years.

Top left: What Air Force One is to the President of the United States, the DeHaviland DHC-2 Beaver was to Wentworth's president. The Institute bought the plane in 1973 from the U.S. government's surplus properties division. The plane, built in 1957, was 30 feet long and had a wingspan of 48 feet.

Bottom left: Aircraft lab, 1972.

Below: East Coast Aero Tech student, 1987.

The ECAT facilities at Hanscom Air Field.

Wentworth Institute of Technology expanded in other ways during the 1980s. In 1986, Sylvania donated its for-profit school, Sylvania Tech, to Wentworth. The Lexington-based organization, renamed Wentworth Technical Schools, offered courses such as avionics/marine electronics and business machine technology. Also in 1986, the Institute purchased the proprietary school, East Coast Aero Tech, located at the Hanscom Air Field in Bedford, Mass. The school boasted a long history of training aircraft maintenance professionals.

At the time, each acquisition made sense. Aircraft maintenance had long been a staple of Wentworth's curriculum. ECAT seemed to offer Wentworth the opportunity to consolidate its leadership in the field by upgrading its teaching facilities. (After all, there's only so much room to house small aircraft at 550 Huntington.) And WTS seemed a chance for Wentworth to stay true to its roots (and Arioch's dream) of providing hands-on education to working-class men and women in technical fields.

Neither venture, however, met with much success. ECAT more often than not ended up on the losing end of sagging aircraft maintenance trends, and a severe blow was dealt in October 1994 when ECAT controller Robert O'Keefe was convicted on 133 counts of embezzling and laundering more than one million dollars from the school. Wentworth sold East Coast Aero Tech for $700,000 on March 20, 1996. As for WTS, its enrollment numbers never came close to the level that would justify what the administration increasingly felt was a dilution of Wentworth Institute of Technology's image. The college no longer wished to be associated with a for-profit school that advertised on UHF television stations during weekday afternoons. Wentworth Technical Schools closed its doors for good in August 1996.

Neighbors Through the Years

No college exists in a vacuum. A school lives in a neighborhood, and a neighborhood means neighbors: apartment dwellers, churches, taverns, public works institutions, even other schools. For the past 100 years, Wentworth has forged countless "town-gown" relationships with its neighbors. A few prominent ones include:

NORTHEASTERN UNIVERSITY

More than just geography links Wentworth Institute of Technology and Northeastern University. Founded in 1899 a couple of blocks up Huntington Avenue, Northeastern has been many things to Wentworth over the years: neighbor, sometimes a role model, sometimes a competitor. Perhaps most often, however, a complement: for many years, Northeastern's programs presented a natural finish to Wentworth's offerings. In fact, close to 2,000 Wentworth two-year graduates went on to earn their baccalaureates at Northeastern. (Wentworth trustees George Chamillard, IE '58, John Kelleher, AET '61, and George Chryssis, EET '69, are three examples.) The institutions have long enjoyed a good relationship with each other, going so far as to share resources. These days, for example, Northeastern's field hockey team makes use of Sweeney Field and Wentworth's ice hockey team does likewise with Matthews Arena.

Northeastern University's Ell Hall.

Mission Main then
and now.

MISSION MAIN

When the city built the Mission Main housing development in 1941, it was considered state of the art. That shin-
ing reputation wore off quickly. In the 1960s, a rundown
dinginess took hold of the project that borders Wentworth
along Ward Street. Its 38 three- and four-story red brick
buildings, housing 1,300 residents, deteriorated into urban
blight. By the early 1970s, the physical decay was mirrored
by the project's descent into one of the most crime-ridden
neighborhoods in the city. For many years, Wentworth
mingled uneasily with Mission Main. The low point, at
least symbolically, came in the late 1960s when the
Institute bordered its campus with a barbed-wire fence.
Presidents Kirkpatrick and Van Domelen, however,
steadily built a good-faith relationship with the community. Over the past three decades, Wentworth and Mission
Main have collaborated on scores of neighborly initiatives,
such as Camp Tech, Dunk the Vote, and Technology Goes
Home. In 1999, the city of Boston rebuilt the Mission
Main complex entirely. The resulting quilt of pastel-
colored townhouses now stands as a showcase of public
housing done right.

PUNTER'S PUB

College students being college students, the facility most
fondly remembered by innumerable Wentworth alumni is
not the library, the cafeteria, or the strength of materials
lab. It's an unassuming, dark-paneled, one-story building
at the corner of Parker Street and Huntington Avenue.
Equidistant from the Northeastern and Wentworth campuses, Punter's Pub is the prototypical college tavern. Since
1971, it has been the place to unwind after a week of final
exams, to share war stories about co-op labors, or to celebrate a Friday night victory by the hockey team. And like
many collegiate pubs, Punter's is an institution that engen-
ders from its alumni a loyalty nearly as fierce as that which
they hold for their alma mater. The pub even holds its
own reunions, which are invariably well attended.

If a Wentworth sports
team won a championship,
you're sure to find its
picture hanging behind
the bar at Punter's.

Fenway Park, before the Monster seats were built in 2003. With a pair of binoculars, students in Wentworth's 610 Huntington Avenue residence hall can follow the action on the center field scoreboard.

Fenway Park

Perhaps the most beloved, and tortured, of Boston's historic landmarks, the home of the Boston Red Sox opened the same month (April 1912) that Wentworth Institute was wrapping up its first year of classes. A ten-minute walk from the Wentworth campus, Fenway Park was for a long time the refuge of choice for hooky-playing Institute students. Especially between 1950 and 1967, when afternoon games were the norm and plenty of seats were always available at Fenway. As fearsome a presence as President Beatty may have been for truant students, the lure of a day in the bleacher seats was often impossible to resist. Put it this way: when Ted Williams stepped to the plate at Fenway Park and stroked a home run in his final at-bat at 3:50 p.m. on Wednesday, September 28, 1960, chances are at least 20 Wentworth students witnessed it firsthand.

The 560 Huntington Avenue firehouse, Wentworth's neighbor for 70 years.

560 Huntington Avenue Firehouse

In the days following the tragic events of September 11, 2001, Wentworth students presented a heartfelt thank-you card to the firefighters who work in the shadow of Williston Hall. One student wrote, "I saw firsthand how awesomely you guys handled the events of 9-11. It was inspiring to watch." The brick firehouse has stood at the corner of Huntington Avenue and Ruggles Street since 1933, home base to Engine 37, Ladder 26, Car 5. These days, as more and more students choose to live at Wentworth, the presence of a crew of Boston's Bravest just seconds away offers a comfort impossible to measure.

Simmons College, one of
Wentworth's partners in
the Colleges of the Fenway
consortium.

COLLEGES OF THE FENWAY

Wentworth Institute of Technology resides in a neighborhood packed not only with world-renowned hospitals and
cultural institutions, but also colleges. In 1996, Wentworth
teamed up with four other schools—Emmanuel, Simmons,
Wheelock, and Massachusetts College of Pharmacy—to
found a consortium called Colleges of the Fenway. (Mass.
College of Art signed on three years later.) By combining
resources with those of its counterparts, Wentworth gives
its students the chance to register for courses to which
they would not otherwise have access, be it Japanese or
Psychology of Selling. The consortium has also helped dis-
pel social stereotypes that once abounded on either end of
the Fenway: Simmons and Emmanuel, for instance, are no
longer home to the stuck-up sisterhood, just as Wentworth
is no longer home to a rabble of roughnecks who wear
workboots to a mixer.

ANNUNCIATION GREEK ORTHODOX
CATHEDRAL OF NEW ENGLAND

The Annunciation Cathedral opened its doors to parish-
ioners on Christmas Day, 1924. For the past 80 years, it
has served as the house of worship in the city of Boston for
members of the Greek Orthodox faith. Built on the corner
of Parker and Ruggles Streets, the cathedral's distinctive
dome offers a graceful backdrop to Wentworth campus
vistas. Over the years, the relationship between the cathedral and Wentworth has been, on the whole, quiet and
respectful. The Institute built Sweeney Field, for instance,
in such a way as to respect sightlines from Huntington
Avenue toward the Annunciation Cathedral.

Annunciation Cathedral at
the corner of Parker Street
and Ruggles Street.

What's that smell? It's the Ward Street Headworks, which looks innocent enough from the exterior. The Mission Church is visible in the background.

WARD STREET HEADWORKS

Every now and then, a ghastly odor wafts through the Institute grounds. The unpleasant scent is the product of an unremarkable-looking facility that squats behind a chainlink fence on the southwest border of campus. The Ward Street Headworks is the transfer station that routes much of the state's wastewater on its way to the Deer Island treatment plant in Boston Harbor. Conspiracy theorists on campus have long hypothesized that Headworks employees take special care to vent their foul gases on days—graduations or open houses, for instance—when the Institute is thronged with visitors. Whether that's true or not, the Headworks for decades have taught Wentworth students two important life lessons: One, the world doesn't always deal you the best hand. Deal with it. And two, learn how to breathe through your mouth. It's just easier that way.

Top: The Huntington Avenue residence and machine shop originally owned by Warren E. Collins.

Above: The most famous product to emerge from Collins' workshop, the iron lung.

COLLINS BUILDING

In 1966, Wentworth Institute purchased a three-story brick building on the north side of Huntington Avenue. In the years since, it has served many purposes for the Institute: Russ Beatty kept an apartment on the upper floor; the Curriculum Center called it home, as have the Alumni Office and the Career Center. But of all the work done in the building, the most famous was performed by its original owner, Warren E. Collins. He was a mechanical manufacturer who lived on the top floor and ran a machine and assembly shop on the lower floors. In 1928, he partnered with Philip Drinker, a chemical engineer and industrial hygiene professor at the Harvard School of Public Health. Drinker had developed a model for a machine to sustain the breathing of polio patients who suffered paralyzed pulmonary functions. Collins and Drinker manufactured the first of hundreds of tank respirators at 553-555 Huntington Avenue in the late 1920s. Most everyone, however, came to know the machine by its less formal name: the iron lung. In the decades before the Sabin-Salk vaccine was developed, the iron lung saved the lives of many patients afflicted by polio.

The Museum of Fine Arts was built in 1908, the same year Wentworth's directors purchased the campus grounds. In Arioch Wentworth's first will, written in 1887, he saw fit to bequeath $100,000 to establish a Wentworth Wing in the museum, which at the time was located in Copley Square. The bequest disappeared when he rewrote his will in 1903.

MUSEUM OF FINE ARTS

For 95 years, Wentworth Institute of Technology and Boston's Museum of Fine Arts have stood sentry on opposite sides of Huntington Avenue. The two institutions are not natural allies; the MFA with its high-culture aesthetic and WIT with its blue-collar, technical bent. But by this point, it's nearly impossible to imagine one without the other. For many years, Wentworth ushered visitors to its campus through an ornate brick entryway directly across the street from the MFA's signature piece of outdoor art: Cyrus Dallin's "Appeal to the Great Spirit" sculpture, which depicts a Native American chief on horseback. Willard Merrill, MC&TD '37, recalls registration day in September 1935 when he took the bus from Portsmouth, N.H., to South Station in Boston. Suitcase in hand, he walked from the station toward Wentworth Institute: "I was whistling, skipping, and looking up as I studied the tall buildings. Approaching Wentworth, I first climbed the stairs of the Museum of Fine Arts and in the company of the Indian I spent a few minutes gazing across the avenue enjoying the view of Wentworth and its surroundings."

1990

THE VAN DOMELEN ERA, 1990-PRESENT

Top left: Dr. John F. Van Domelen, Wentworth's third president.

Left: Wentworth Hall, right, and Dobbs Hall, left, along with Williston Hall, regained their prominence as centers of academic life in 2000 when the Institute renovated the facilities and built connectors on the upper levels.

Below: Whether in a lab or on a lap, computers are omnipresent on the Wentworth campus today, as Justin Ragsdale, BMT '05, illustrates.

With Ted Kirkpatrick's retirement imminent, the trustees in 1989 began the search for Wentworth Institute of Technology's third president. They selected John F. Van Domelen, vice president for academic affairs and dean of faculty at Norwich University.

When Dr. Van Domelen arrived at Wentworth in 1990, he found an institution in good shape, if worn around the edges. Outmoded laboratories and studios posed a problem. The president jokes, "We still had outsized electrical machinery that when started up, tended to black out the Boston skyline." John Van Domelen set about improving the Institute at a time when a demographic crisis loomed and the competition to enroll students grew fiercer by the year.

Three prominent trends weave their way through the Van Domelen era.

A Full-Fledged Four-Year School

One is the full flowering of Wentworth Institute of Technology as a baccalaureate institution. By the mid-1990s, the associate's degree had become a means, not an end, at Wentworth. Only three percent of the students who entered Wentworth in 1994 intended to depart with just an associate's degree in hand; 33 percent intended to finish with a bachelor's degree; and 57 percent set their sights on a terminal degree higher than the baccalaureate.

Wentworth's new concentration on the bachelor's degree paid no disrespect to the Institute's longstanding tradition of offering two-year certificates and degrees. Instead, it reflected the school's typically close attention to the culture and practices that reign in the workplace. In the 1980s, engineering technology employers, especially those in the Northeast, started to lose faith in the associate's degree. As industry grew more and more high-tech, the bachelor's degree became the entry ticket to virtually every profession around which Wentworth's academic programs were oriented.

Board Chairman Robert Boyden understood well this progression, having experienced a similar circumstance at Wentworth 40 years earlier. Boyden had received a certificate in machine construction and tool design in 1952. Five years later, his alma mater—having just rewritten its charter—contacted him and his classmates to see if they were interested in taking supplementary courses to upgrade their certificates to associate in engineering degrees. Boyden, along with scores of other graduates from the early '50s, jumped at the opportunity—the academic equivalent of trading in an old car for this year's improved model.

Above left: President John Van Domelen and Robert Boyden, MC&TD '52, in 1998, moments before Chairman Boyden received an honorary doctor of engineering technology degree.

Left: Professor Peter Philliou demonstrates the properties of air flow during an Open House presentation in the Project Laboratory.

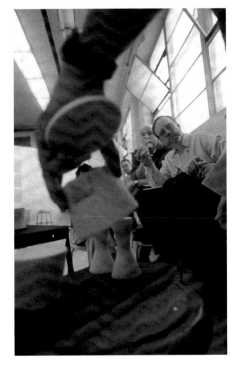

Design disciplines have grown increasingly popular at Wentworth during the past 15 years.

Clockwise from above: Industrial design critiques teach Wentworth students to operate under pressure, as they present their work to a panel of faculty members and design professionals.

The architecture studio, a beehive of creative activity.

Late nights in the studio are a rite of passage for interior design, industrial design, and architecture majors.

Industrial design began in 1990; interior design five years earlier. The latter is a professional degree program accredited by the Foundation for Interior Design Education Research.

Five-year engineering majors began in 1993.

Above: Electromechanical engineering seniors Kurt Bruck, left, and Paul Balutis built a robot, Artoo, that learns by means of a neural network. In 2002, their project won first place at the American Society for Engineering Education's student competition in West Point, N.Y.

Top: Environmental engineering students Steven Nabozny, left, and Stephen Reichenbacher work on their capstone senior project in the spring of 1999. Their project focused on remediation of the polluted Muddy River in the Fenway.

The full embrace of bachelor's degrees during the '90s reverberated throughout the Institute's academic structure. The curriculum needed some tinkering. Whereas the associate's track had been like a 100-yard dash, the bachelor's track equated to running a 10K road race. On one hand, this opened up opportunities for Wentworth. For instance, it allowed the school to incorporate in a more satisfying fashion the 20 percent allotment of humanities and social science courses that has become the standard in engineering technology education.

But it also created challenges. Because Wentworth students declare their majors upon entering as freshmen (most schools defer this decision till the close of a student's second year), the Institute had to make sure that core courses didn't get trampled in the rush to specialize. This challenge grew more complicated due to cooperative education; students need to have been sufficiently exposed to their discipline before beginning co-op in the third year. And then there's the student entering her junior year who expects a seamless transition when she decides to switch her major to industrial design after having studied architectural engineering technology the first two years. These are a few reasons why crafting a robust and efficient curriculum is an extremely difficult task.

The best solution to the above challenges? Van Domelen's decades of service within two famously bureaucratic operations—the military and higher education—made him a disciple of simplification. (The president knew red tape when he saw it. He'd been on the other side of the looking glass, including the time at Norwich University when he served on the Committee on Committees.)

Organizationally, his Wentworth became leaner than it had been in decades. When he arrived in 1990, Wentworth's academic division was a complicated stew of colleges and departments. Within two years, Van Domelen disbanded this bureaucratic quagmire and replaced it with a model of seven departments, each with a head who reports to the provost. The majors that the school offered also reflected a renewed trimness. In 2003-04, the Institute offered 16 degree programs; 20 years previously, there had been 29 programs, including some short-lived misfires such as dental laboratory technology.

Simplicity did not mean an end to innovation, however. Two new majors that debuted in the '90s pioneered a new era at Wentworth Institute of Technology. In 1993, the school introduced a pair of five-year majors, environmental engineering and electromechanical engineering. These were professional engineering programs, a big step forward for the Institute. Engineering demands a different approach than engineering technology; much more attention needs to be paid to the theoretical underpinnings of a subject, not an easy transition for a school as relentlessly practical as Wentworth. In 2002, the Engineering Accreditation Commission accredited these two programs, an independent affirmation of the quality of the offerings, and an approval that allows graduates to sit for professional engineer's registration exams.

EDUCATION THAT WORKS

Over the years, Wentworth Institute of Technology has enjoyed especially strong bonds with certain employers. Today, you can find scores of companies and firms where a Wentworth diploma seems to be practically a job requirement. In some respects, cooperative education has reinforced this close alliance between Wentworth and some employers. But even before co-op, plenty of companies relied on Wentworth to serve as their failproof feeder system.

In 1957, for instance, the Boston structural engineering firm, Cleverdon Varney & Pike, had 85 men on staff. Of these, 18 were Wentworth Institute alumni; or 19, if you count the fact that one of the partners, Robert Cleverdon, received aviation training at Wentworth during the war years. Half of the six partners came from the Institute, and three out of the five structural project managers were Wentworth men. About these project managers, partner Herbert Albee, AC '37, wrote in 1957: "Dick Hirth, AC '47, is number one man under the chief engineer and he carries several projects at once….Ken Avery, AC '40, is quiet but extremely thorough. When he goes over a job it's been gone over….Elias Joseph, AC '50, is a real buzz saw when it comes to digging in and 'let's get going.'" In addition to the job captains, Albee noted a "number of excellent designers and draftsmen from Wentworth who are climbing up the proverbial ladder." To top it off, Cleverdon Varney & Pike also employed four former Institute instructors.

The Digital Equipment Corporation also established an extensive network with Wentworth graduates. Founded in 1957 as a three-person operation in Maynard, Mass., Digital grew to 800 employees by 1965. That year, 38 of those employees held degrees from Wentworth Institute. Almost every one of them had graduated in the last six years from the electronic engineering technology program. It was the start of a beautiful relationship: each year, Digital laid out the welcome mat for a handful of the top graduates from the EEE program, and each year these "best and brightest" were delighted to hook up with one of the hottest high-tech companies in the country. From that point, the Wentworth/Digital connection only grew

stronger. In 1991, Digital estimated that one percent of its huge workforce had graduated from Wentworth. Jack Smith, IE '58, is a noteworthy representative of the Wentworth/Digital family. When he left Digital in 1993, he had risen all the way to chief operating officer; he received the Wentworth Alumni Association's highest honor, the Gold Leopard Award, in 1991.

Wentworth's electronic engineering technology program was the Triple-A feeder system to Digital Equipment Corporation's "major league" team in the '60s. This 1965 photo shows 31 young Wentworth graduates who had signed on in the preceding few years with Digital.

These days, construction firms often get into bidding wars with each other not only to land big contracts, but also to land the brand-new graduates from Wentworth Institute of Technology. The Gilbane Building Company in Providence, R.I., has managed to recruit an impressive share of Wentworth grads. In 2003, more than 40 Wentworth alumni work at Gilbane—ranging from Richard Famiglietti, AET '63, and Robert Manocchia, AET '64, who are, respectively, an estimating executive and district manager, to Jason Goodwin, BCMT '02, who's an office engineer. Project manager Dan Lanneville, CMC '97, points out what draws Gilbane to Wentworth grads: "The Institute trains us for exactly what we end up doing in the workplace. Gilbane doesn't have to 'unteach' everything we've learned. Because Wentworth professors carry practical experience, graduates are ready to go from day one."

39. George T. Balich
The Architect

Wentworth Institute of Technology has come a long way academically in the 15 years that Dr. George Balich has been provost. Before being

appointed as the chief academic officer in 1988, Balich had taught architecture at Wentworth for 12 years. The provost's background as an architect has come in handy as provost: Balich has performed an impressive renovation of the Institute's educational structure. He has assembled a faculty that's the most accomplished in the school's history. The Institute's 16 academic programs have received a wide assortment of approvals from accrediting agencies. And he has shepherded the entry of engineering programs into the Wentworth curriculum with the 1993 debut of the five-year majors, environmental engineering and electromechanical engineering.

40. Robert W. Boyden, MC&TD '52
The Molder

Trustee Bob Boyden embodies the way Wentworth Institute of Technology has come of age in the last decade. For the Institute's first 88 years, an "outsider" led the board of trustees. Not that this was a bad thing—the 11 board chairmen

up to 1992 were an extraordinary group of leaders. Nevertheless, these were men whose life experiences tended more toward the Harvard Club than toward pouring molten iron into molds. That ended in 1992 when Boyden became the first Wentworth alumnus to ascend to the board's chairmanship. A 1952 graduate of machine construction and tool design, his father Howard was an alumnus as well (MC&TD '27). Bob possessed two qualities especially useful to a board chairman: courage and strategic savvy. The former he showed as a decorated fighter pilot in the Korean War. The latter he developed as founder and president of Boyden Molding Inc., a thriving Taunton-based plastics company. (For years, Boyden was the world's most prolific builder of hotels. His firm manufactured Monopoly's game pieces.) The vision the chairman molded for his alma mater was strongly

informed by his perspective as an alumnus. He wrote in 1993, "It bothers me when people say the United States cannot compete in the world market. That's nonsense. This country used to be the world's technology leader. There's no doubt in my mind that Wentworth holds the key: the hands-on approach is our strength, and it's just what this country needs."

41. Dan Lanneville, CMC '97
The New Breed of Student

Dan Lanneville represents the new breed of student who has begun to enroll at Wentworth during the last decade. That is, the high-caliber student whom colleges fight over. Wentworth won

the fight for Lanneville. In 1993, he arrived at the Institute as a member of the first class of Arioch Scholars, academically accomplished students awarded lucrative merit scholarships. He could have chosen Roger Williams University or the University of Maine. He chose Wentworth instead. "The Roger Williams construction management program seemed much too theoretical," he says, "and even though UMaine offered me a nice scholarship, the Arioch Scholarship tipped the scales toward Wentworth." He lived up to his reputation at Wentworth, not only as a student (he graduated with a 3.99 GPA) but as a leader, serving as president of the Student Government Association. The presence of students like Dan Lanneville has helped raise Wentworth's profile nationwide. Today, Lanneville works as a project manager for the Gilbane Building Company of Providence, R.I., one of the country's top-10 contracting firms.

42. Francis Nestor
The Teacher

It's a cardinal rule of planning a wedding: never waste an invitation on someone who isn't important in your life. Now, consider that Frank Nestor, a professor of mathematics since 1966 and longtime basketball coach, has attended 20 alumni weddings over the years. No faculty member in Wentworth's history has ever forged a tighter bond with students. Nestor accomplished this both in the classroom and on the basketball court. In the classroom, his successes have been unfettered. He has the uncanny ability to turn calculus—historically a black hole for students—into a "can't miss" class. In the gymnasium, he racked up successes just as impressive—in every

area but wins. Nestor holds the NCAA coaching record for taking the longest time to win 100 games at one school. "But he always understood

the big picture," says one of his players, Andre Vega, ARC '96. Behind the scenes, Coach Nestor ushered Wentworth into NCAA ranks in 1984. He has been honored with every major award bestowed at Wentworth: the Grant Johnson Award for outstanding teaching in 1980, the Gold Leopard from the Alumni Association in 1995, and induction into the Athletics Hall of Fame inaugural class in 2001.

43, 44. Eugenia and Myles Sweeney, AC '28
The Benefactors

It's tempting to call Myles Sweeney a prodigal son. But in reality, he never left the fold of his alma mater. He just stayed quiet for 67 years. His busy career had something to do with that. A 1928 architectural construction graduate, Sweeney worked for 33 years at the Johns Manville Corporation. There he developed new technology relating to sound isolation and reverberation control. During the 1940s, he built sophisticated wind tunnels for the agency that would become NASA. In 1993, a retired Sweeney reconnected dramatically with Wentworth. He had seen an advertisement about charitable

remainder trusts in the alumni magazine, so he called Dick Burtt, vice president for development, to inquire about it. He and his wife, Eugenia, wanted to donate land they owned in Bedford, Mass. The couple did just that, netting Wentworth proceeds of approximately two million dollars—the single largest contribution to the institution since Arioch Wentworth's founding bequest. The Institute used the funds to build the Myles Elliott and Eugenia Louise Sweeney Field on the long-undeveloped plot of land at the corner of Ruggles Street and Huntington Avenue. Myles Sweeney died shortly before the field opened in 1996. Eugenia Sweeney, however, has continued the family's philanthropic legacy. In 2000, she contributed $350,000 to upgrade Sweeney Field with a press box, concessions stand, changing rooms, and other enhancements.

45. John F. Van Domelen
The Community Builder

Wentworth is an institution defined by its presidents. H. Russell Beatty and Edward T. Kirkpatrick each put an unmistakable stamp on the school during their respective long tenures. Dr. John Van Domelen has done the same in his 14-year presidency. He has steered the Institute with much the same philosophy that powers his championship-caliber golf game: Keep it straight and simple. Trust the clubs in your bag. Don't lay up. And play to win. A retired Air Force colonel who served in the Vietnam War, Van Domelen arrived at Wentworth in 1990 after serving as vice president for academic affairs and dean of faculty at Norwich University. In short time, he and the trustees crafted an ambitious vision statement for the Institute titled, *By the Year 2000*. Some of the goals seemed far-fetched at the time, the institutional equivalent of holing out a 75-foot putt. Nevertheless, by the time the year 2000 arrived, Wentworth marked a birdie on its scorecard—practically all of its goals had been met, allowing the Institute to enter the 21st century stronger and healthier than it had ever been before. Highlights of the Van Domelen era have included the introduction of two accredited five-

year professional engineering degrees, an array of other accreditation successes, the reinvigoration of student life on campus, and the relentless upgrading of laboratories, facilities, and faculty qualifications. The 2001 opening of the residence hall at 610 Huntington Avenue highlighted what may eventually be regarded as President John Van Domelen's greatest accomplishment: building a vigorous sense of community on campus.

46. John Vetere, BCS '78, CE '81
Co-op "Poster Boy"

"I'm sort of the poster boy for the cooperative education program," John Vetere joked in 1998. As a civil engineering technology student 20 years earlier, he completed his first co-op semester as a sewer inspector for the Massachusetts

Water Resources Authority. That co-op set in motion a tide of career fortune that crested in 1997 when the MWRA promoted Vetere to direct its Deer Island wastewater treatment plant. A multibillion-dollar facility forged by a federal mandate to clean Boston Harbor, Deer Island is an engineering marvel. Each day, the plant treats 370 million gallons of wastewater from 43 Greater Boston communities. Vetere is the man responsible for its smooth operation. And though it may be far from fragrant, his career represents a classically elegant use of a Wentworth education.

47. Robert Villanucci, EEE '66
The Homegrown Professor

Bob Villanucci is a standout example of a venerable fraternity of Institute faculty: the homegrown

Wentworth professor. Villanucci, who graduated in 1966 with an associate's degree in electronic engineering technology, joined the faculty in 1970 after receiving his bachelor's degree from Northeastern University. He has taught at the school ever since. The author of four electronics textbooks, he twice earned the Grant Johnson Award, given each year to an outstanding faculty member at the Institute. Villanucci has held the Henry C. Lord Chair since 1999, and remains one of the key architects of the Institute's thriving electromechanical engineering program. He also has established himself as perhaps the most active researcher among Wentworth's faculty. A recent project involved developing and testing the validity of a computer-based algorithm that uses wavelet transform techniques to detect the presence of a medical condition called ventricular tachycardia.

48. William N. Whelan, EEP '63
The Chairman

When Bill Whelan headed the Boston real estate development firm, Spaulding & Slye Colliers, he grew to hate the long commute from his New Bedford home. So, he found a different route. Through the air. After gaining a pilot's license, he bought a twin-engine Cessna 414 and set about reclaiming the thousand-plus hours each year

that had been wasted in Route 24 gridlock. It's all about focus, explains Whelan: "Wentworth helped focus me when I was a student. Since

then, my strength has always been my ability to laser-focus on a goal and keep focusing until it happens." It's this clear-eyed, problem-solving attitude that guides Wentworth Institute of Technology as the school enters its second century. The board of trustees appointed Whelan as chairman in September 2000; he succeeded another alumnus, Robert Boyden, MC&TD '52.

49, 50. Alan and Robert Whittemore, S&DE '47
The Wentworth Family

Wentworth history is writ large in the careers of the father-and-son team, Robert and Alan Whittemore. The two men have contributed a combined 73 years of service to the Institute. Bob graduated from the steam and diesel engineering program in 1947, and immediately began a 41-year career at his alma mater; Alan began his 32nd year in 2003. Between them, they taught mechanical engineering technology for four decades, admitted students to the Institute,

coached the baseball team to two junior college championships, ran the registrar's office, gained entry into the Athletics Hall of Fame, managed curricular programs for evening and weekend students, won the Grant Johnson Award for teaching excellence, and conjured a hockey program to life at Wentworth. (That would be, respectively: Bob, Alan, Bob, Alan, Bob, Alan, Bob, and Alan.)

A Changing Student Body

The second trend of the Van Domelen era is the changing profile of the students who enroll at Wentworth.

Each president of Wentworth has taken a different view of what constitutes the perfect number of enrolled students. Ted Kirkpatrick aimed high. In 1981, he set the long-term goals as 5,000 day students by 1985, and 7,000 by 1990. The enrollment grew considerably, but still fell 1,000 students short of the 1985 goal.

Van Domelen, by contrast, concluded that the law of diminishing returns applied to student enrollment at Wentworth Institute of Technology. Taking into account the constraints of a 35-acre urban campus, combined with the desire to keep classes at a size where the professor can know every student's name, he calculated 2,800 day students as a more sensible target to aim for.

For a few years in the mid-'90s, however, even this more manageable number seemed a mockery. Wentworth faced the same problem that threatened hundreds of other colleges nationwide: a shortage of 18-year-olds. Population experts called it a demographic trough. College administrators called it a crisis. From year one to year six of President Van Domelen's tenure, the Institute saw a 30 percent drop in student enrollment. Wentworth pulled through impressively, though. Unlike many other colleges, it survived the bear market without laying off a single employee.

By 1997, Wentworth classrooms had started to fill to capacity again. Just as heartening was the type of student now sitting in these classrooms and laboratories. Not to mention the type of student who *wasn't* sitting in there. The Institute had started to shape its incoming classes with a more discriminating eye. By the late '90s, Wentworth's Admissions Office had taken to rejecting unqualified applicants—a new phenomenon at the Institute.

Wentworth and its insurance carrier grew to dread each other's calls in the flood-ridden fall of 1996. Two fierce Northeasters—the first on September 18, the second on October 20—triggered overflow from the nearby Stony Brook conduit and Muddy River. The September storm sent water rushing into 12 campus buildings and caused classes to be cancelled for three days. The October storm was even worse. Eleven inches of rain fell in a 36-hour span, pouring water relentlessly into 20 campus facilities. The Annex on Parker Street was especially hard-hit. Power systems campuswide were knocked offline, school was closed for five days, and Physical Plant employees worked 24-hour days for an entire week to combat the flood and its aftermath. Damage was $8 million. (And the school suffered another $4 million in damage after a June 1998 storm.)

Below: On October 20, 1996, Steve Powers, left, and Jose Laboy, rear, saved computers in the basement of the Annex from a soggy end. The water level was two feet high when this photo was taken at three in the afternoon. It rose another foot as the day wore on.

Below right: The quad became Lake Wentworth for a day.

By recruiting applicants more selectively, the quality of incoming students rose noticeably. Average SAT scores spiked from 830 in 1990 to 1067 in 2003. A high school valedictorian or two started to roam Wentworth's halls. Wentworth alumni have long identified their alma mater, affectionately, as a "school for C students." And that was mutually understood to be an honorable role. Today, the best aspects of that tradition remain alive and well at Wentworth. It's just that now a lot more A and B students are mixed in.

Financial aid is one means by which Wentworth Institute of Technology has convinced outstanding students to attend. Merit awards such as the Arioch Scholarship, which grants $10,000 a year to academically qualified students, have paid off great dividends for the school. "Arioch Scholars are like yeast that makes all the dough rise," says Professor Amos St. Germain.

Financial aid has been a priority for President John Van Domelen. At his inauguration in 1990, he said, "We do not have a national policy of supporting the education of the next generation of technologists, engineers, or scientists, and that contributes to the lack of interest that young men and women have for those career fields." Lacking a national policy, Wentworth strengthened its institutional policy. The Institute increased its financial aid awards tenfold during the '90s. In 2003-04, 75 percent of day students received some aid from the school. The average award package totaled $7,800.

Karin Stewart, a 2001 construction management graduate, worked her senior-year co-op with Bond Brothers Inc., an Everett-based general contractor who built Wentworth's residence hall at 610 Huntington Avenue. Here, Stewart monitors the progress of the construction in November 2000. (The dorm opened nine months later in August 2001.)

As effective a lure as money provides, the greatest inducement to attend a school is its reputation. During the past 15 years, Wentworth's national reputation has grown steadily. For most of its history, the school had been quite provincial. Ninety percent of its students came from Massachusetts, and the rest were mostly within a 90-minute drive—Rhode Island or southern New Hampshire and Maine.

The student population today, while not quite cosmopolitan, does originate from a broader geographical spectrum. Massachusetts supplied 52 percent of the Class of 2007. Ten percent of the class came from New York and New Jersey, and students hailed from 22 states in all.

And with what colleges does Wentworth Institute of Technology compete? Because the school occupies a unique niche, there's no simple answer. Many students who are attracted to Wentworth also apply to Northeastern University. (And, historically, Northeastern also happens to be the institution where close to 2,000 Wentworth alumni earned their bachelor's degrees.) Sometimes the competition depends on the major in question. For instance, a student who wishes to pursue a bachelor of architecture degree in the Northeast might look at Roger Williams, Rhode Island School of Design, and the Boston Architectural Center, in addition to Wentworth. A student interested in computer science has more choices, but might add schools such as Suffolk University or UMass Lowell to a list that includes Wentworth.

A Sense of Community

Perhaps the most sweeping change witnessed at Wentworth during the Van Domelen era has been the growing sense of community on campus. Student life at Wentworth today is markedly different than it was as recently as 20 years ago.

For example, consider a cool evening on October 3, 2002, when 100 Wentworth students sat in the bleachers of Sweeney Field to watch the varsity women's soccer team notch a night-game victory over UMass Boston. Just a typical fall evening on the Wentworth Institute of Technology campus of the 21st century. But read that first sentence again. At least three things occur that were inconceivable at the school 20 years ago.

There's no question that college students learn as much outside the classroom as they do inside it. For decades, however, Wentworth provided precious few opportunities for extracurricular enrichment. Some older alumni remember their alma mater as "the Factory" or "Wentrock." You sprinted from the train to make your 8 a.m. class, then hustled from classroom to lab to lunchroom back to classroom again, never daring to disrespect the heavily regimented schedule. By the time 4 p.m. finally rolled around, you weren't really eager to "enrich your extracurriculars." Frankly, you were just looking to get the hell out of Dodge. The notorious "forced fun" period offered only meager comforts. No surprise, then, that many Wentworth alumni reflect on their college days not so much with fond and wistful nostalgia, but rather with the sort of grim, teeth-clenching recall that's more often associated with one's first hump-busting, full-time job.

This fate resulted from Wentworth's entrenched no-frills personality and its commuter school status. Both of these attributes, however, have diminished during the last decade of the 20th century and the first few years of the 21st.

2001-02 was a milestone year. Commuting day students numbered 1,208 that year; 1,505 day students lived in Wentworth housing. For the first time in the history of the school, more students slept on campus than away from it.

The lure of the 610 Huntington Avenue residence hall that opened in August 2001 had something to do with the shift. Housing 473 students, appointed with luxuries that made parents envious, and wired with a vengeance (President Van Domelen liked to boast that the dorm features "three portals per pillow"), the new hall immediately established itself as the centerpiece of Wentworth's reinvention as a residential school.

Similarly, the other major building project of the Van Domelen era, Sweeney Field—an artificially surfaced soccer/softball/lacrosse field on the corner of Huntington and Ruggles—symbolized a surging commitment to organized intercollegiate athletics at Wentworth Institute of Technology.

Each year, Wentworth Institute of Technology reaches out to the community by hosting or participating in scores of different programs and collaborative initiatives. Recent examples include a day of community service performed by 1,200 Wentworth students; Project Strive, an on-campus recycling program that employs dozens of special-needs students from the Boston school system; and Technology Goes Home, a program that provides computer training, lab space, and ongoing support for low-income families.

Even with 30-plus hours of classes and labs, there's still occasional time for Ultimate Frisbee on the quad.

Wentworth has turned into a predominantly residential campus over the past decade. The Institute features four residence halls on its campus. And another is slotted to be built on the north side of Huntington Avenue in the next few years. When the new dorm goes online, Edwards/Rodgers Hall (built in 1924) will be given a well-deserved retirement.

Clockwise from above: A fifth-floor study room in the 610 Huntington Avenue residence hall offers a great view of the Back Bay skyline. When the dorm opened in August 2001, it marked the first time in Wentworth's history that resident students outnumbered commuters.

Move-in day, 2000.

Both the Edwards/Rodgers and 610 Huntington dorms feature kitchens.

A freshman hauls luggage toward his Evans Way room.

THOSE CRAZY DAYS OF COLLEGE

Wentworth, let's face it, has never been mistaken for a fun house. For much of its history, the Institute was run in a very controlled, almost domineering manner. Some alumni joke that the reason Wentworth performed so well both times the government asked it to administer wartime training programs, was that it was, essentially, already a military school.

Principal Williston, for instance, monitored student attendance with a ferocity that made Grand Inquisitors seem laid-back by comparison. Principal Dobbs sought salvation in bulletin boards. Each week he assaulted Wentworth students with a new posting to announce the latest prohibition on campus: no smoking on the stairs, no loud voices in the hall, no driving off campus grounds at noon. Dobbs also stood frequent vigil in the parking lot, waiting for the school van to return from an athletic event. As the student-athletes got off the van, the principal made spot inspections of their gym bags. Anyone caught with a towel sporting another school's initials found himself cleaning up the foundry for the next month.

These two principals, however, merely served as a warm-up for the true master of the craft. President Beatty turned oppressive paternalism into an art form. David Gannon, AM '56, who entered the Marine Corps in 1956 two months after graduating from Wentworth, jokes, "To me, Marine boot camp felt like a vacation at a luxury resort compared to Wentworth. It felt strange all of a sudden to have so much freedom and relaxation, and not have to worry so much about people breathing down your neck every minute of the day."

Anyone who suspects Gannon's comment to be an exaggeration never sat through a Beatty-era convocation. These assemblies, which occurred with alarming frequency, turned Watson Auditorium into a hall of horrors for many a Wentworth student. First came roll call; attendance was mandatory at these events, and heaven help the late arrivers, never mind the no-shows. Next came the "deportment examination;" any students slouching toward Bohemia with respect to facial hair received immediate attention in the form of a one-on-one counseling session. And if all that wasn't enough to break your spirit, then came the kicker: Mrs. Beatty would start singing.

The "Wentrock" image started to soften once Presidents Kirkpatrick and Van Domelen hit the scene. Which is not to say that the Institute has turned into a mecca of laughs and merriment. That would be nearly impossible at a school with a workload as punishing as Wentworth's.

Nevertheless, students through the years have found a way to inject some fun into Wentworth Institute of Technology. And what's more, their shenanigans frequently reveal a hands-on cleverness that is intrinsically Wentworthian.

George Gramatikas, BCS '78, ME '79, made Wentworth's 1978 Spring Commencement one to remember. He masterminded a prank that became known in Wentworth circles as "The Fotomat Incident." Earlier that year, the Institute had erected a security kiosk at the entrance to the West Parking Lot. A few days before commencement, George and a group of classmates fashioned a striking likeness of Fotomat's distinctive hut roof, using canvas, Styrofoam, and strips of wood. When the morning of commencement arrived, the group snuck their creation onto the back of a pickup truck and parked in a nearby alley. Families of the graduates, meanwhile, had begun to park in the West Lot. (Ceremonies were held at the Hynes Auditorium that year, so Wentworth was shuttling attendees from the campus.) Once the coast was clear, Gramatikas' crew executed a military-style operation to drive the truck back to campus and hoist the roof into place atop the kiosk. They had just completed the mission when the shuttle buses returned from the Hynes. It turns out the group's handiwork was quite convincing. About ten different families pulled up to the kiosk as they drove out of the parking lot, and dropped off the film containing the photos they had just snapped at the Hynes. So, if you're still looking for your developed prints from the 1978 commencement, please contact George Gramatikas, CEO of Turbine Technology Services in Orlando, Fla.

In the early '90s, John Q. Alumnus (the statute of limitations for his offense has yet to run out) and his roommates showed a similar hands-on solution when it came to enlivening their residential experience at Wentworth. John was part of a large group of friends;

four of them lived in one suite in the Evans Way residence hall, the other four lived in the suite next door. They were a close-knit bunch—the two groups always ended up spending most of the time hanging out in one suite. Unfortunately, common rooms in these suites weren't designed to accommodate eight young men comfortably. So, they proposed a simple idea among themselves: Why not remove the interior wall that separated one suite from the other? In fact, it seemed so simple an idea that the men deemed it not worthy of bothering the Housing Office with the details. With the volume of their stereo turned up just high enough to drown out the SkilSaw's racket, the offending wall came down. (The students disposed of it in small chunks over the next few weeks so as not to arouse suspicion.) For the rest of the year, the eight friends had a terrific time together in their suddenly spacious suite. When the year drew to a close, the suitemates smuggled in some studs, drywall, and plaster, and restored the cavernous suite back to its original two-suite status. The Housing Office never caught wind of the renovations. In hindsight, we can be grateful that at least one building construction major in the suite must have paid attention during the class that dealt with load-bearing walls.

Both of these examples, in a bizarre way, illustrate the fruits of Wentworth's application-based instruction. The final example, however, makes no such claims; we include it solely as a public service. One weekend night in 2002, some Wentworth students, who shall remain nameless, lugged a dorm-size refrigerator onto the roof of Tudbury Hall, approximately 100 feet above street level. For whatever idiotic reason, the students launched the fridge airborne and watched as it crashed down to the sidewalk at the main entryway. Then they carried idiocy to a whole new dimension. They filmed the entire fiasco on a Webcam, and proceeded to download it onto the Internet! Needless to say, it didn't exactly require Sherlock Holmes-like skills of detection for Wentworth's dean of students to ferret out the perpetrators' identities on Monday morning. The moral? To paraphrase Dean Wormer's immortal words to Bluto Blutarsky in the 1978 classic, *Animal House*: "Son, drunk and stupid is no way to go through life."

Above: George Gramatikas, BCS '78, ME '79, left, and a cohort took trademark infringement to new heights with the infamous "Parking Lot Prank of '78."

Top and top right: How many engineering technologists can fit into a phone booth? Students from Wentworth College of Technology's 1974 class did their best to come up with an answer.

Wentworth, home of champions.

Below: Men's lacrosse became a varsity sport in 1997.

Bottom left: On November 2, 1996, Coach Sean Murphy, left, and Chip Swarner, AEC '98, celebrated the soccer team's Commonwealth Coast Conference championship victory on brand-new Sweeney Field.

Bottom right: In recent years, center-ice celebratory pileups have become an expected end-of-season occurrence for the ice hockey team. Starting in 2000, the Leopards appeared in four consecutive ECAC Northeast championship games, and won three of them.

Sports had always had a place at Wentworth. Intramural games had long been a fiercely contested component of the lunch-hour break. At an intercollegiate level, baseball dates back to 1914 and riflery began a few years after. The football team had an abbreviated but glorious run from 1933 to 1951. [*See story on Page 78.*] During the '50s, '60s, and '70s, Wentworth competed in baseball and basketball against local junior colleges. They even won a couple of junior college baseball championships in the '60s under Coach Bob Whittemore, S&DE '47. But, for the most part, athletics were a subdued affair at Wentworth Institute.

That changed in 1984 when Professor (and then Dean of Students) Frank Nestor convinced the administration to apply for Wentworth's membership in the National Collegiate Athletic Association. Some wondered at the time if he was a glutton for punishment. After all, Coach Nestor had a hard enough time defeating basketball teams *not* at the NCAA-level.

With NCAA Division III membership in place, most of Wentworth's varsity teams joined the Commonwealth Coast Conference. The Institute added more sports in the '80s, including men's soccer and women's basketball. But the only team to enjoy much success during the decade was the baseball team, which won CCC titles in 1989 and 1990.

Up to the mid-'90s, Wentworth teams tended to be league doormats. Coach Nestor, for example, tasted not a single winning season during his 15 years as men's basketball coach. The men's soccer team went 1-17 in 1995. And the ice hockey team endured a dismal 50-game losing streak in the mid-'90s.

But the hiring of a few full-time coaches, mixed with a little old-fashioned stick-to-it-iveness, ended Wentworth's doormat days. The baseball team went to the

ECAC postseason tournament in 1995, and knocked off top-seeded Amherst College in the first game. The 1996 men's soccer team, inspired by their new home, Sweeney Field, scored a surprising Commonwealth Coast Conference championship. Men's basketball won consecutive CCC championships in 1997 and 1998, and secured an invitation in 1997 to the prestigious NCAA Division III tournament. And the hockey team came back from the dead to win ECAC conference championships in 2000, 2002, and 2003, earning NCAA tournament invitations all three years as well.

New athletic programs sprang to life with encouraging results, too. Women's soccer arrived in 1998 and within five years became one of the best programs in the Northeast, and men's lacrosse and golf also joined the roster in the mid-'90s, bringing Wentworth's varsity sports menu to eight men's teams and five women's teams (plus riflery, which is coed).

Assistant to the President Ron Betts sums up the motivating principle behind the sporting revival at Wentworth: "Our interest in athletics is based on the belief that our students would not have a well-rounded college experience either as players or as fans, if their teams didn't have any chance of succeeding on the playing field. It's all part of spirit, memory, and engagement."

So, whether it's new dorms, new sports teams, or new attitudes, the overriding result has been an unprecedented sense of community at Wentworth. The 9-to-5 mentality is a thing of the past—Wentworth now ticks on a student's clock. Which means, for all intents and purposes, the campus never sleeps. Students who are on the Mini-Baja team tinker at all hours in the project laboratory in Kingman Hall. Movie night packs them in every Thursday night at the Annex Auditorium. And the lights never seem to go out in the architecture studios.

Below: On February 27, 1997, Coach Harry McShane, right, and members of the men's basketball team exulted after the first of their two consecutive conference titles.

Below right: Members of Wentworth's Mini-Baja team combine mechanical ingenuity with a passion for off-road driving. The 2001 national Mini-Baja competition, shown here, took place in Troy, Ohio.

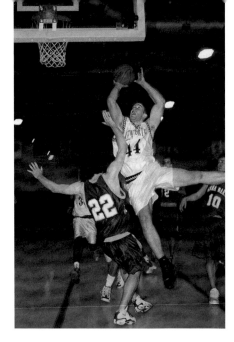

The sporting life at Wentworth is richer now than at any time in the school's history.

Clockwise from top left: There's no stopping Greg Altavilla, BMT '05, in a 2003 game against Anna Maria College.

In 2003, the women's softball team enjoyed a best-ever 19-15 record.

Rugby has been a popular club sport for many years.

Barry Lopes, BCM '03, rips a corner kick on Sweeney Field.

Four Wentworth sports stars in the past decade have garnered the premier honor given to student-athletes: a spot on the Academic All-America Team: Matt Bouchard, ARC '97, baseball; Kevin Hanlon, BCT '00, basketball (two-time member); Jamie Weiss, BMT '03, hockey (two-time member); and Sarah Bearse, BELM '05, soccer.

Why Leopards?

In the '30s and '40s, Wentworth's intercollegiate sports teams were known as the "Technicians." Today, however, Wentworth's mascot is the leopard, which begs the question of why. The answer lives in triplicate on the Institute's official seal, where a trio of leopards stare balefully at the viewer.

The Institute adopted its coat of arms from its founder, Arioch Wentworth, whose family shield dated back to the 13th century. William Wentworth of Yorkshire, England, fashioned it. Later, when Thomas Wentworth became burgess of Oxford in 1603, the University College honored him by placing in its refectory a stained-glass window that featured the Wentworth shield. The colors were black and gold. (Unfortunately, Wentworth Institute's founding directors had been unaware of this color scheme. When the school opened in 1911, Principal Williston chose black and cardinal red as the school colors. It stayed that way until 1928, when faculty member Raymond Thompson caught sight of the Wentworth stained-glass window during his vacation in England. When he reported his find to Mr. Dobbs, the principal switched the official school colors to black and gold. In a nod to the first few decades, however, red stayed on as the color of the chevron in the school's seal.)

The 1969 Wenitech student newspaper gamely laid forth the symbolic import of the leopard to Wentworth students: "This valiant warrior signifies such traits as bravery, swiftness, triumph, and engagement in hazardous enterprises."

In May 2003, Wentworth Institute of Technology unveiled a dramatic six-foot-high leopard sculpture in its residence hall plaza on Huntington Avenue. The most hazardous enterprise this "valiant warrior" now faces is the steady stream of camera-toting families looking to snap a shot of their sons and daughters at what has become the campus' top photo-op stop.

Above: Three leopards, each bearing an enigmatic expression, have emblazoned the Wentworth family crest since the 1200s.

Below: The 2003 dedication of the Wentworth leopard sculpture.

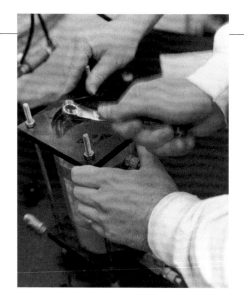

Still Hands On After All These Years

What exactly does "hands-on" mean? It's a philosophy that dates back to the founder's belief that one learns best by doing. Arioch Wentworth had himself apprenticed in the soapstone trade. While he saw flaws in the apprenticeship system, he dreamed of founding a school that would succeed by adopting its best aspects. So, from day one at the Institute, students didn't learn about pattern making by reading textbooks. Instead, they actually made patterns.

Associate Provost Nick Boas describes the philosophy in this way. He points out that when Wentworth Professor Tom Taddeo earned his bachelor's degree in civil engineering from Tufts University, not once did he lay eyes on a transit or a total station. But tools such as these are a staple of the academic diet at Wentworth. A traditional engineering school teaches as if it anticipates its graduates will never leave the office. Wentworth, on the other hand, teaches as if it anticipates its graduates will always be right where the work is happening, while it's happening.

During the 2002 academic convocation, Professor Robert Villanucci, EEE '66, told students about the difference between the kind of education he received at Wentworth and the kind he received elsewhere:

Below: In March 2002, eight teams of industrial design students built disaster relief shelters on the quad. As part of the project, each team spent a cold and rainy night in their respective shelters.

Below right: Soils and foundations laboratory, 2000.

"In all the coursework that I took after Wentworth, only one engineering course had a laboratory component. And that was only three nights! Done. You know, if it weren't for Wentworth, I would have received very little practical experience from any of my formal education. The amount of time you students will spend in the studios and labs will be far more than what your friends will experience—friends who have chosen to go to other colleges and universities. From this practice-oriented education, you develop a kind of 'knowing confidence' that allows you to think that even though you have not seen something, you can still work it out because you can draw from a wealth of practical experience."

CHALLENGES AHEAD

Challenges remain, however. One that forever faces the administration is how to keep tuition as low as possible. Wentworth Institute of Technology has always been one of the least expensive private colleges in Massachusetts. Its 2003-04 tuition, $15,000, is 42 percent less than the price tag of its next-door neighbor, Northeastern University.

The Institute's endowment plays a big part in the administration's ability to keep tuition relatively low. Despite a rough patch in recent years, the endowment has still nearly doubled in value during President Van Domelen's time at Wentworth. In 1990, the value was $35 million; by 2003, it had grown to $64 million.

Student retention stands out as an area for improvement. More than a third of students who enroll at Wentworth drop out before earning a degree. The reasons are many. For one, a Wentworth education is specialized and intense, so it tends to spin away uncommitted or unfocused students with a powerful sort of centrifugal force. But that explanation doesn't solve the problem. One of the four keywords on the Institute seal is "economy," and poor retention of students offends that sensibility because it drains Institute resources, be they human, financial, or spiritual. To address the problem, President Van Domelen convened a retention task force in 2000. On the bright side, administrators expect that the school's increasingly residential character will encourage students to stay the course where they might not have before.

But the Institute's greatest challenge in the coming years remains the same one that has faced the school for 100 years: to take the hundreds of young men and women who arrive each fall and teach, train, cajole, badger, and shape them into practical-minded, sure-handed, technically savvy, solution-driven professionals. The school's success rate in meeting this challenge remains unblemished.

Wentworth Institute of Technology may not have invented hands-on technical education. But, over the course of the last 100 years, no other school has come closer to mastering it.

Professor John Cooper advises management of technology students. Wentworth is one of only a handful of colleges nationally to offer an accredited bachelor's degree in management of technology.

Who Are Wentworth Alumni?

Who are Wentworth alumni? Nearly 40,000 men and women have graduated from the Institute during the past 92 years. Some general conclusions we can make about them: They're doers, fixers, and builders; the ones you want on the front line when it comes time to solve a problem. They're practical-minded, energetic workers. They're productive citizens, contributing their technical and technological know-how to improve the world they live in. And they're leaders, active in their fields and communities.

Following are several examples of fields that have been enriched by the contributions of Wentworth alumni.

CEOs

Of course, Wentworth alumni know how to run a turbine engine, a CAD program, or a cement mixer. Turns out they also know how to run a business. Thousands of Wentworth alumni serve as the chief executives of their company/firm/corporation; many of them founded the business in the first place.

For instance…

Robert Swanson, PET '59, is chairman of the board of Linear Technology Corporation in Millpitas, Calif., one of the leading firms in the high-tech nexus of Silicon Valley. Since Swanson founded LTC in 1981, the company has been one of the world's foremost manufacturers of semiconductors, averaging $500 million in sales in recent years.

In a similar field is George Chamillard, IE '58, who rose through the ranks in a 35-year career at Teradyne Inc., a seven-billion-dollar semiconductor testing firm. In 1997, the Teradyne board promoted him to chief executive officer. Two years later, The Boston Globe awarded him its "Bang For Your Buck" CEO of the Year award.

George Chamillard, IE '58, chief executive officer of Teradyne Inc.

John Fuller, BCS '77, is the founder and president of Boston-based Fuller Associates Inc., a midsize architecture firm with a diverse portfolio of corporate/commercial, hospitality, educational, and residential clients.

Jane Estella-Minias, AET '75, a member of the first class of women to study at Wentworth, runs Artios Associates, an architecture/interior design firm in Boston.

CONSTRUCTION MANAGERS

Thumb through the Yellow Pages to scan the hundreds of construction companies that serve the Greater Boston area. At virtually every one, you'll find at least one Wentworth graduate in the management ranks.

For instance...

Cosmo Pallazola, CHE '60, is senior vice president of Modern Continental, one of the largest construction companies in the Northeast. He contributed as much expertise to Boston's Big Dig as any individual involved with the $16-billion project.

Karen Arpino, AET '79, is a senior project manager at SEA Consultants Inc. in Cambridge; she's a leader in the planning of building projects. Formerly, she was the director of design and construction for the MBTA.

Peter Rizutto, CHE '65, is senior vice president and general manager of the Perini Corporation, one of the top-20 contracting firms in the United States.

GOVERNMENT SERVANTS

Politics may make strange bedfellows, but it's not all that strange that some Wentworth graduates have carved out successful careers as elected government officials. After all, politics transpires in much the same way as, say, mechanical engineering. You study a problem. You weigh the various resources at your disposal. You administer the solution in the most efficient and potent way possible. You move on to the next problem.

U.S. Congressman Stephen Lynch, CMW '88.

For instance...

John Volpe, AC '30, is Wentworth's most famous alumnus, a reputation earned on the merits of a Horatio Alger-type political career. After 25 years as the head of a successful construction company, Volpe was chosen by President Eisenhower to lead the Federal Highway Administration. He returned to Massachusetts in 1960 to serve the first of three terms as governor. In 1969 he left the State House to join President Nixon's Cabinet as Secretary of Transportation. He ended his career as ambassador to Italy.

Stephen Lynch, CMW '88, also entered the political arena after years of laboring in the building trades. He was an ironworker until an on-the-job injury persuaded him to earn a law degree. In 1994, he won a seat in the Massachusetts House of Representatives; two years later he jumped up to the State Senate. In 2001, Lynch won a special election to the U.S. House of Representatives, filling the 9th Congressional District seat of the deceased Joseph Moakley.

ENGINEERING TECHNOLOGISTS

Engineering technology has long been Wentworth's calling card. The Institute graduates professionals who occupy the front lines of engineering projects and challenges. And we should all sleep easier for that fact. Put it this way: When you drive over the Leonard P. Zakim Bunker Hill Bridge in Boston, you'll take comfort in knowing that many of the project's surveyors, field engineers, and construction supervisors happened to be Wentworth engineering technology graduates.

For instance…

Marc Menard, AET '74, is a nuclear examiner at the Portsmouth Naval Shipyard in New Hampshire.

Patrick Piwowarski, BCC '90, works as a machinist for Conrail Railroad in Nashua, N.H.

George Papaioannou, AET '62, came out of retirement in 2002 to coordinate the building of a reverse-osmosis water treatment plant in Naples, Fla.

MILITARY OFFICERS

The values on the Wentworth seal are "Honesty, Economy, Energy, System." Perhaps no field relies more on these principles than the military. No surprise, then, that the U.S. Armed Forces feature a long list of Wentworth graduates who boast exemplary service at high ranks.

For instance…

Brigadier General Loring Astorino, IEC '56, is the highest-ranking military officer in Wentworth history. General Astorino enrolled in the U.S. Air Force three months after graduating from Wentworth. He served for the next 34 years. After receiving his pilot wings in 1958, he went on to compile 6,500 flying hours. In Vietnam, he flew 147 combat missions in B-52s. His military decorations include the Legion of Merit, Distinguished Flying Cross, Meritorious Service Medal with oak leaf cluster, Air Medal with six oak leaf clusters, and Air Force Commendation Medal with oak leaf cluster. He ended his tenure with four years as commander of the 7th Air Division, Strategic Air Command, Ramstein Air Base, West Germany.

Navy Commander Stephen Crane, MED '62, served three tours in Vietnam, completed 155 missions as a Navy fighter pilot, and made 752 carrier landings during his 25 years in the service. In the early '80s, he qualified as one of 200 pilots vying for a place in NASA's space shuttle program, but narrowly missed being selected as one of the final 36. Having retired from the Navy in 1986, Crane now teaches math in a special education program at Pensacola High School in Florida.

BUILDING INSPECTORS

Walk into the Town Hall in any one of the 351 communities that make up the Commonwealth of Massachusetts. Odds are one in three that the building inspector or building commissioner graduated from Wentworth. It's a job that taps into the real strengths of a Wentworth education. A good building inspector is a hands-on pro who understands the building trade from a broad variety of perspectives and who knows every trick behind what separates a first-rate structure from an inferior one.

For instance…

William Gedraitis, AET '62, has been building commissioner for the town of Middleboro, Mass., for 27 years. In 2000, he was honored as Outstanding Building Official of the Year in Southeastern Massachusetts.

Kathleen Nugent, AEC '85, is one of several Wentworth grads involved in building inspection for the city of Quincy, Mass.

After retiring in 1992 as an environmental engineer with the Commonwealth's Department of Environmental Protection, Frank Addivinola, PM&MD '49, signed on as a building inspector in Franklin, Mass. Over the next 10 years, nearly 2,000 houses in the town were built or renovated under his watchful eye.

INVENTORS

Wentworth graduates are a self-sufficient breed; they prefer to do things for themselves. If they can't find what they want in the marketplace, then they're apt to invent it. What is it that makes Wentworth alumni such an inventive lot? It has a lot to do with the fertile combination of a curious mind and capable hands.

For instance…

Russell Colley, MC&TD '18, played a part in putting man on the moon. Of the 65 patents Colley developed for the B.F. Goodrich Company, the most noteworthy invention turned out to be the silver nylon space suit that Mercury astronaut Alan Shepard wore on the first manned space flight on May 5, 1961.

Luther Blount, MC&TD '37, is a prolific inventor of nautical, mechanical, and even medical devices. His first patent came in 1949 for a catamaran hull; more than 50 years later, boat designers continue to use the design. Other inventions, such as the bow boarding ramp, the retractable pilot house, and the pint-a-flush toilet offer testimony to how Blount's inventive genius has fed his lifelong success as a boatbuilder and cruise line mogul.

Should your car ever break down on Route 495 in Massachusetts, you might very well benefit from the 30-year-old invention of John DeGiorgio, EEE '66. He dreamed up the emergency call boxes that dot highway roadsides—a Good Samaritan innovation that has grown somewhat less necessary since the onslaught of cell phones, but no less ingenious.

Above: Luther Blount, MC&TD '37, christens his pint-a-flush toilet, 1989.

Russell Colley, MC&TD '18, claimed that a tomato worm inspired his space suit design.

ARCHITECTS

For the past 15 years, Wentworth Institute of Technology has sent architects out into the design world; and before that the school boasted a long record of preparing men and women to matriculate elsewhere and earn their architecture degrees. Wentworth-trained architects have the reputation of being strong not only on design, but also uncommonly tuned-in to the latter half of "design/build."

For instance…

David Stirling, AET '68, and Les Brown, AET '65, run the award-winning firm, Stirling/Brown Architects, in Winchester, Mass. They've designed more than 130 projects in Winchester alone, and received much media attention in 2002 with appearances on the Home & Garden TV show, *Before and After,* and PBS' *This Old House,* as well as an article in Boston Magazine.

As additional proof that two Wentworth heads are better than one: Charles Cramer, BC '68, and Howard Levine, AE '74, are the founding partners of the thriving firm, Cramer Levine & Company, Architects, in Easton, Mass.

James Garvin, AET '63, is not a registered architect, but instead a remarkably passionate and eloquent spokesman for the field in his role as the official architectural historian for the State of New Hampshire. He has published numerous works, including the 2001 book, *A Building History of Northern New England.*

Irene McSweeney Woodfall, BCS '83, CEC '85, CE '88, of the Boston Water and Sewer Commission.

ENGINEERS

While the lifeblood of Wentworth has long been engineering technology, the Institute in recent years has started to stake more of a claim to straight engineering as well.

For instance…

Steven Bernstein, BC '68, brings an engineer's sensibility (he holds a master's degree in environmental engineering) to his role as president of the Daylor Consulting Group in Braintree, Mass. Daylor offers advanced technology solutions for land planning. In 1982, the Massachusetts Society of Professional Engineers named Bernstein Young Engineer of the Year.

Robert Chagnon, MC&TD '57, is a professional engineer who consults on structural engineering issues. He received the Engineer of the Year Award in 2003 from the Delaware Engineering Society.

Irene McSweeney Woodfall, BCS '83, CEC '85, CE '88, makes productive use of her civil engineering background in her role as director of construction for the Boston Water and Sewer Commission.

David Stirling, AET '68, of Stirling/Brown Architects.

EDUCATORS

In a satisfying sort of lifecycle, Wentworth's faculty has always been heavily populated by Wentworth graduates. As it turns out, a great many Institute graduates go on to become teachers at all educational levels. It makes sense; Wentworth puts great stock in its hands-on philosophy, and the most hands-on job in the world may be that of teacher.

For instance…

David Stevens, EEE '66, has taught mathematics at his alma mater for the past 30 years. Winner of the Grant Johnson Teaching Award in 2001, he's also the author of numerous math textbooks.

After 22 years as a foundry manager for the Hathaway Machinery Company in New Bedford, Mass., J. Gerin Sylvia, APM '32, made the leap to teaching. He ran the foundry department at Wentworth from 1958 to 1969, then moved on to teach industrial engineering at Pennsylvania State University, West Virginia University, and the University of Rhode Island. In 1972, he wrote *Cast Metals Technology*, the leading textbook in the field.

Rosalie Williams, CSW '86, teaches computer science in the Cambridge school system.

Wilfrid Savoie, EEE '64, dedicated his professional life to improving vocational education. He retired in 2001 after 25 years as superintendent-director of the Blue Hills Regional Technical High School in Canton, Mass.

UNCOMMON ENTERPRISES

Wentworth takes great pride in its outstanding track record of graduating men and women into careers closely related to their courses of study. Nevertheless, exceptions to the rule exist. And these exceptions support the thesis that while Wentworth's education may be tightly focused, by no means does it prevent graduates from the successful pursuit of a broad array of career aspirations.

For instance…

Dr. Otley Dugan, EC '35, is one of a very small group of Wentworth alumni who went on to become medical doctors. The good Dr. Dugan brought most of the residents of Swanton, Vermont (pop. 6,203), into this world.

Gregory Portukalian, BCS '74, has put his building skills to especially elegant use as a violin dealer in Providence, R.I.

Similarly, Robert Eddy, BCS '78, has carved out a unique niche as a model yacht maker in Camden, Maine.

George P. Castano, PM&MD '39, is a retired reverend of St. Peter's Episcopal Church in Denver, Colorado. Amen.

Robert Eddy, BCS '78, with one of his custom model yachts, 1993.

THE NEXT ERA: WENTWORTH INSTITUTE OF TECHNOLOGY IN THE 21ST CENTURY

As a benefactor, Arioch Wentworth had the touch of Midas. All three of the institutions he founded near the end of his life—the Wentworth Home for the Aged, Wentworth-Douglass Hospital, and Wentworth Institute of Technology—continue to thrive 100 years later.

Despite having reached such an advanced age, though, Wentworth Institute of Technology still has room to grow—physically, academically, and socially. The first era of Wentworth's second century, therefore, offers opportunities for as many advances and as much progress as any of the previous eras witnessed.

The Institute's trustees and president have elaborated a plan detailing the way this progress will play out. At the turn of the century, the administration developed a vision statement titled, *By the Year 2007*. The goals are ambitious but well within grasp. Some, in fact, have already been grasped.

President John Van Domelen presents the case for why Wentworth Institute of Technology matters in this day and age: "Technological education is critical to the United States' role in the world economy and its position as a leader in manufacturing, construction, and design innovation. The education offered at Wentworth guarantees its graduates the ability to participate in the nation's accomplishments and to have an impact on technological progress, the quality of the built environment, and manufacturing excellence throughout the world."

Left: The Recreation Center, one of several building projects on the Institute's drawing board. Intended for the corner of Parker and Prentiss Streets, the rec center will offer, among other things, Wentworth's first home hockey rink. (For many years, Wentworth has leased ice time at Northeastern University's Matthews Arena.)

Below: The proposed Information Technology Center, which will be a centerpiece of 21st-century academic life on the Wentworth campus. The new facility will reside where Edwards/Rodgers Hall currently stands.

How Does Wentworth Plan to Improve?

Many of the admissions goals in the plan are quite reachable, and might be considered more a forecast of where already-upward trends will plateau. The quality of admitted students will continue to escalate—the average combined SAT score will be 1050 (*mission already accomplished: it was 1067 for students entering in the fall of 2003*). Half of the students will come from outside Massachusetts (*almost there: 48 percent did this year*). And women will make up one quarter of the entering class (*still a ways to go: they made up 19 percent this year*).

Perhaps the biggest challenge among the admissions goals is student retention. The plan states, "Wentworth will graduate 60 percent of its incoming undergraduate students with the baccalaureate degree within six years." The rate, which has climbed slowly during the past decade, reached 54 percent in 2003. The 60 percent goal has sparked a renewed commitment to counseling, financial services, and enhancing every aspect of the student experience at Wentworth—especially during the crucial freshman year.

Academically, the focus is to remain on the vanguard of technology. This is familiar territory for Wentworth—the rule for any technology school is to stay innovative, or perish. This applies to pedagogy, course content, and the integration of co-op into the curriculum. Also, if history is any guide, Wentworth Institute of Technology will have to develop new courses of study during the next decade. The test for the Institute is to choose the right ones.

A pillar of the plan that offers the most room for progress is the goal to become nationally recognized. Wentworth's strengths are well known regionally, but much less so outside of New England. The plan states, "Recognition will be the result of active student, alumni, and faculty involvement, and their personal success at the national, regional, and local levels of professional, educational, and civic organizations." The theory is that Wentworth's reputation rises an inch or two higher every time electromechanical engineering students win an American Society for Engineering Education competition in West Point, N.Y.; every time a computer science alumnus enrolls in MIT's graduate program; and every time a professor wins an award for work on a bridge renovation, or authors a linear integrated circuits textbook, or travels to Los Angeles to present a scholarly paper on software engineering.

Wentworth's physical plant will offer the most visible signs of improvement during the Institute's next decade. Four new or renovated facilities are on the drawing board:

- Information Technology Center;
- Recreation Center, featuring a hockey rink;
- Transforming Beatty Hall into a true campus center; and
- A 300-bed residence hall.

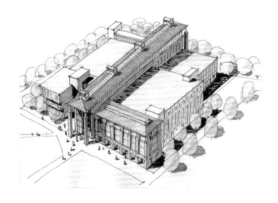

Once the Information Technology Center is built, Beatty Hall will transform into a comprehensive Student Center. This aerial perspective offers a look at one scenario, which incorporates a dramatic common area between Beatty Hall and the Nelson Recreation Center.

The Institute is in the midst of a $30-million capital campaign, Building the Future, to raise the funds to support these projects, in addition to bolstering the Institute's endowment and annual fund.

What then is the end result of these various goals contained in Wentworth's *By the Year 2007* vision statement? Simply, the fulfillment of Wentworth Institute of Technology's mission to be the "premier provider of practice-oriented undergraduate programs in the fields of architecture, computer science, design, engineering, technology, and the management of technology, as well as innovative continuing education programs for full-time working professionals."

Arioch Wentworth would be proud to see not only how far his institution has traveled, but also how close it's remained to his dream.

Some recent representatives of the nearly 40,000 beneficiaries of Arioch Wentworth's dream to furnish education in the mechanical arts.

PHOTO CREDITS

Robert Arnold, Fabian Bachrach, Amos Chan, Joseph Clifford, Dave Desroches, John Earle, FayFoto, Patrice Flesch, Jack Foley, Gustav Freedman, Steve Fusi, Globe Newspaper Company Inc., Dana Heller, Bill Johnson, Justin Allardyce Knight, Richard Mandelkorn, William Mercer, Bill O'Connell, Perkins & Will/Shaw (architectural renderings on Pages 168-70), Jim Rinaldi, Tony Rinaldo, Len Rubenstein, Russ Schleipman, Steven SetteDucati, Merrill Shea, William Short, George Simian, Stephen Spartana, Thomas Stevens (Providence Journal-Bulletin), William Thuss, Joshua Touster, U.S. Library of Congress, Melina Vanderpile, Peter Wrenn.